WISDOM
TREASURES

WISDOM TREASURES

Ageless Riches for A Modern Society

TERRENCE D. RICHBURG

PALMETTO
PUBLISHING

Charleston, SC
www.PalmettoPublishing.com

Wisdom Treasures

Copyright © 2020 by Terrence D. Richburg

All rights reserved.
No portion of this book may be reproduced, stored in a retrieval system, or transmitted in any form by any means–electronic, mechanical, photocopy, recording, or other–except for brief quotations in printed reviews, without prior permission of the author.

Printed in the United States of America.

Hardcover ISBN: 978-1-64990-279-5
Paperback ISBN: 978-1-64990-278-8

Dedication

I'd like to take this opportunity to dedicate this book to the many people I have had the preordained blessing to know, whether they were in my life from the very beginning, or if I had the amazing privilege of having our paths cross—while on the road to seeking, obtaining, and experiencing the apex of true wisdom and enlightenment in Jesus Christ, my Savior and Lord.

These wonderful souls have blessed my life with sound counsel, real-life exampling, and profound inspiration, to seek the purity and power of spiritual wisdom directly from the source—Jesus Christ, the expressed Living Word of God, and the embodied sum of all wisdom, entirely wise and undeniably omniscient!

These include my dad, John E. Richburg; my mom, Wilhelmina S. Richburg; my paternal grandmother, Ellen Richburg; my maternal grandmother, Ella Burke; my uncle, Julius Richburg; my former late pastor Rev. John D. Bussey of Bethesda Baptist Church in Washington, DC; my friend and former pastor Rev. A. Michael Black, then of Bethesda Baptist Church in Washington, DC; my current pastor, Rev. Dr. Ricky D. Helton of Israel Metropolitan CME Church in Washington, DC; my devoted friends and supporters from the Lord Dr. Jerry West and his wife, Vee, of Israel Metropolitan CME Church in Washington, DC; my prophetic and encouraging friend Bishop Al Way of Faith Assembly of Christ Church in Washington, DC; my very close friend and confidant Rachel Hall; my close friend and witness for the Lord Ronald Smith; my beautiful wife and gift from the Lord Kathy Richburg; and so many others both young and old who have knowingly or unwittingly shined the pure light of true wisdom and trusted counsel into my heart and spirit.

SPECIAL DEDICATION

A gifted young talent of amazing proportions, Daniel Levon Hall—a very dear friend of mine and the brother of my goddaughter Tameka—tragically passed away during the time I was completing this book. Though he was taken from us so suddenly, we know that his life and music exemplified a deep trust in, knowledge of, and reverence for God, with no fear in his heart to live life to the fullest. He was wise beyond his years in his gift of music and in the profound messages he brought to this generation and beyond. We will sorely miss him.

So, I'd like to especially dedicate this book to Daniel, the Hall family, and to Daniel's legacy. He made the wisest decision of all: to fully commit his life no matter how brief to his family and most notably to the Lord, Jesus Christ! Rest on in peace, my dear brother. We'll see you again!

And to all, I say, I love you and I thank you!

Blessings always,
Terrence

TABLE OF CONTENTS

Foreword ix
Introduction xiii
Chapter 1   The "Piggy Bank" Effect 1
Chapter 2   Once upon a "Switch" 3
Chapter 3   The Real Fear Factor 10
Chapter 4   Looking Forward—The Magnitude of Wisdom 15
Chapter 5   The Paradox of Fear 18
Chapter 6   Transitioning from Fear to Wisdom's Power 20
Chapter 7   Assessing Ageless Wisdom versus Contemporary Understanding 25
Chapter 8   God's Revelation of Spiritual Wisdom 32
Chapter 9   Pursuing the Mind of God 37
Chapter 10   Shifting to a Childlike Wisdom—A Supernatural Power .. 46
Chapter 11   Reexamining the Relationship of Fear and Wisdom 54
Chapter 12   You Have Not Because You Ask Not—Where Is Your Wisdom? 57
Chapter 13   Surveying Wisdom's Glorious Treasures 60
Chapter 14   Practical Wisdom for a Modern Society 63
Chapter 15   The Anti-Wisdom War Movement 74
Chapter 16   So, Where Do We Go from Here?—The Takeaways 89
Chapter 17   Challenging Questions for Challenging Times 96
Chapter 18   Just for Fun... 98
Chapter 19   Closing Thoughts and Hopes 103
References (Online) 107
About the Author 115

FOREWORD

"Oh no, not another book on wisdom!" That was my initial reaction when I opened up the email and saw the title of the manuscript. *Wisdom Treasures*. But knowing Terrence Richburg, as I have come to know him and his beautiful wife, Kathy, this would not just be another wisdom book to put on my shelf. My "Oh no" would become "Oh yes."

What compels world-class artists and musical geniuses in the caliber of Stevie Wonder, Victor Wooten, Quincy Jones, and Terrence Richburg to write a book outside of their musical niche on a subject as complicated and controversial as wisdom? As a trained theologian, applied scientist, educator, and yes, musician, I recognize the importance of teaching our youth on wisdom literature much in the same vein as would the wise man, priest, and prophet. However, to muster up the courage to write a book about it is beyond my imagination if not capability.

So, what inspired Terrence to write nineteen chapters on wisdom? What inspired him to put down his bass guitar, his pianos, his compositions, his band, and the many pursuits that drive this musical genius and carve out the time to research and write a book about wisdom? That was the question that I kept asking as I made my way through the book. And finally, I got to chapter 19 and there it was. Lo and behold, I was astonished and humbled to no end to discover that he wrote *Wisdom Treasures* largely because I encouraged and inspired him to do so. Wow! To know that my life has had that kind of impact on a person as gifted as Terrence and conversely his on mine—that we both at one time or the other have inspired each other to write books—is truly remarkable. That's really what friends are for. So, it is with great honor and deep humility that I write this foreword for a great friend and brother.

Terrence and I have remained connected through the years in some wonderful events, most of which involve musical collaborations. In August 2010, I along with his newfound sweetheart, Kathy Olatunde, was featured in concert at the Sheraton Hotel in Chantilly, Virginia, along with the Israel Metropolitan CME Church Worship Team. I remember the glow in Kathy's eyes and the joy that exploded out of her mouth as she introduced me to Terrence. When she shared with me that Terrence was a gifted musician, which included giftedness in several musical instruments, I knew that he had won Kathy's heart. Immediately, I began to prepare for the day that I would lose Kathy's beautiful soprano and her powerful spirit. And true enough, in the weeks ahead I watched them unite in marriage and ministry and set out on an amazing journey together that has blessed me and so many in ministry, recordings, concerts, and yes, books—three in ten years.

While I am many years older than Terrence, God placed us on parallel paths. Much of our lives are mirror images. As a result, our relationship has grown over the ten years that we have known each other into a power friendship built on mutual respect and deep admiration. I remember the joy I felt in 2013 when Terrence autographed copies of his first book, *Intimacy: Missing "Peace" in the Puzzle of True Love & Close Relationships*. My wife (affectionately known to Terrence as Vee) and I had just won our battles with kidney and prostate cancer. While reading *Intimacy*, I was inspired to write *EndSanity,* a nonfiction book of my victory over fear of failure. In 2018, Terrence published his second book, *Soul of a Poet's Heart,* a beautiful treasure of poetry, written while Vee was battling breast cancer. I had the pleasure of reading some of my favorite romantic passages from the book to Vee at Terrence's book and multiple CD release event. I will never forget that moment as the tears welled in my wife's eyes as I read from the *Poet's Heart*. Little did I know that a third book was being birthed out of a chapter from the *Poet's Heart* on *wisdom cultures*. And as God would have it, in July 2020, Terrence bestowed upon me the honor to write the foreword to *Wisdom Treasures,* at the one-year anniversary of my wife's successful heart transplant surgery.

What makes *Wisdom Treasures* a must-have book is that it serves to remind us to be constantly aware of our limitations in knowledge. This marries with my beliefs as a lifelong learner and a principle that I live by: *if you learn more, you can do more.* He cautions the rational thinker, the leader, not to waste your life with the meaningless pursuit of knowledge for knowledge's sake. To the Christian, he challenges us to be honest and ask ourselves, When it comes to spiritual things, what do we know? The sad reality is that most will admit that we know very little about spiritual things. This alone is a wisdom treasure.

If you like storytelling, you will love this book. Terrence, like King David, who was also known as a great musician, uses the gift of storytelling and a childlike spirit to provide a practical understanding to his treatment of wisdom. Terrence describes wisdom metaphorically as a "glorious ship that carries on board endless treasures." I chuckled at times as Terrence takes great pain throughout the early chapters to describe himself as "just a normal kid." Try as he may, his definition of normal is obviously different from mine. Growing up in a family of gifted musicians and being recognized throughout your childhood as a child prodigy leading a band is anything but normal.

A final thought. Oh yes! Another book on wisdom. Thank you, Terrence, for giving us *Wisdom Treasures* at a time where people are suffering and need God's wisdom as never before. Thank you for reminding us that there is hope in the midst of our suffering and that hope is found through the fear and reverence of a sovereign God. That is a wisdom treasure to keep for the ages.

Dr. Jerry L. West
EndSanity, 2016, Tate Publishing
Changing Mindsets to Transform Security: Leader Development for an Unpredictable and Complex World, 2013,
Center for Technology and National Security Policy

INTRODUCTION

HAVE YOU EVER BEEN IN a dilemma at work, at a meeting, or at some other company or public event in which you were presumed to be the well-read expert and esteemed presenter to the group? You were rolling right along just fine. You were following your notes to the letter, like a true master orator. You used your hidden slide changer and impressive laser pointer like a pro to highlight all the important stuff on the screen.

Everything was going great! And there were huge smiles for miles all around. But then it happened. Someone in the audience abruptly interrupted you and asked a question that you should have known the answer to, but you didn't. Screech! Oh, my goodness…

Ironically, the question was one that you had never been asked before. In fact, this had never happened to you before—to others maybe, but not to you! This was the defining moment in real time, when you discovered that despite all of your hours and hours of careful preparation and research, somehow you missed something.

And now your naked ignorance was on full display in front of everyone—people who knew you and some that didn't. But they all knew as they sat there seemingly in biblically inspired one-accord-ness, they were in the process of witnessing for the first time your complete meltdown on stage. And there was absolutely nothing you or anyone else could do about it.

You were so embarrassed. So, you tried to deflect and then rebound by using an intelligent-sounding answer—an answer to another question on a different subject on which you were pitch perfect. But unfortunately, it was a question that no one had asked.

So, everyone knew what you were trying to do, as the tenor of your quivering voice along with the proverbial pin-dropping silence, accompanied by the chorus of crickets, filled the impeccable acoustics of the room. Now, all you wanted to do was fade deep into the background and assume a submissive position, seated out of the way in the rear left corner.

It happens. It happens to the best of us. But times like these let us know how vulnerable we are in the pursuit of knowledge. As much as scientists, astronomers, doctors, lawyers, philosophers, and all manner of really, really smart people have learned and discovered, isn't it amazing how little they actually know compared to all there is to know?

When I watch science shows on TV about nature, the earth, and the universe, I always discover something new and amazing. But I often chuckle when I see the presenters and the experts talking among themselves with this superior tone and towering posture. They look and sound as though they know everything about everything there is.

Then I notice that they often use these clever qualifiers like, "it's possible that," or "we firmly believe," or "in all probable likelihood." This tells me that they really aren't sure about what it is they're talking about at all.

But they still want to give the viewers that stone-faced assurance of integrity. However, I submit that the best approach is to assume a posture of humility and clearly acknowledge that you don't even know how much you don't know. That goes for all of us!

But that's not the end of it. Don't wipe your hands clean of the matter and just walk away. There is still a path to all manner of knowledge and understanding available to us. We just need to take the baby steps of humbling ourselves and candidly acknowledging our ignorance.

Then we can set out on a quest to learn from the source of all knowledge. We can resist the urge to simply go it alone or go along with the status quo and follow the popularized message of the crowd—the urge to advocate philosophies with hidden complicity and apathy, rather than fight for the light of truth and its wise application.

It means taking the time to turn off the noise and distractions of those in the public square that would lead you to depreciate the value of evidence-based information and authentic results. It means courageously following a process that absolutely works and leads to all wisdom and truth, especially in terms of our current daily living. But it's also for the benefit of our future survival.

I honestly don't know how people live in a world like ours today, where everywhere you turn there's trouble and pain, and confusion and destruction. It's difficult as it is trying to live when you indeed have God and his direction in your life. But how can people possibly try to live a life without him?

I was fortunate to have had the covering of wise, praying people in my life all around me from birth. But for those who have not, and for those who may have lost their way, how do they even attempt to make wise choices and life decisions in their pursuit of happiness and success?

With this in mind, *Wisdom Treasures: Ageless Riches for a Modern Society* explores the answers to these questions and more. At its heart is the experiential acquisition and biblical legacies of true "wisdom" and its riches. *Wisdom Treasures* examines the details of how wisdom is gained and how its investment or the lack thereof impacts the contour and value of life, from the cradle to the grave.

As an individual or as a community, *Wisdom Treasures* meshes proven truths and ageless proverbs with our modern-day challenge to harvest a lifelong stockpile of assimilated wisdom, and then provide the opportunity to shape it into firm principles to live by and benevolently pass these on to future generations.

Wisdom Treasures also expands upon many of the insights shared in the "Culture of Wisdom" chapter in my book *Soul of a Poet's Heart* and offers a fresh perspective on using the power of spiritual wisdom and understanding to navigate and impact today's society.

CHAPTER ONE

THE "PIGGY BANK" EFFECT

❦

When I write, I find that I'm often drawn back in time to my childhood, as a lens that channels profound light into the various topics I want to discuss and explore. As such, I think one of my fondest childhood memories was my first exposure to banking. Yeah, I know. You heard me correctly. I did say banking!

I must have been around the age of four or five, when my uncle Julius swiftly became my absolute favorite uncle. Why? He used to visit our home quite often to come see my brother and me. But he also rehearsed with my parents to prepare music for the engagements and concerts at which the Richburg Singers, my parents' gospel group, performed.

During my uncle's many visits, he used to call me over to him with a big smile on his face and tickle me to make me laugh. Then he'd go into his pocket, grab my hand, and then shake it while slipping me some quarters, or fifty-cent pieces, or even a dollar bill or two. Sometimes he would even hold out both hands and make me guess which one contained the cash.

My uncle Julius was renowned for giving out money to many of the kids at our family gatherings and events. But when he came over to my house, I was special! And all I could think about when he was there was his continuing tradition, to help finance my vast investment portfolio!

But honestly, at first, I didn't really know what to do with it. The coins just looked shiny, which was kind of cool! And regarding the dollar bills, the exciting oohs and aaahhs from the adults in the room signaled to me that something must be really special about this green-and-white paper I was holding in my hand.

I quickly started to understand more about money and its value when I learned to count it, and especially when my parents gave me opportunities to buy candy from the store for myself. And then the day came when my whole world changed. My parents really took it to a whole new level. They gave me the coveted PIGGY BANK! YES!

Okay, the pig shape was all right I guess, even if the color was very *not* cool. But I really liked the idea of being able to amass a small fortune in my new bank. Plus, my parents told me that one day I could break it open and use the money to buy something huge and important, just for me!

There were times when the whole delayed gratification thing of holding onto all this money, and in a pig, mind you, were not very appealing. But as an aside, after the piggy bank served its useful purpose, I was blessed later with a brand-new bank upgrade—no, not J. P. Morgan or Chase. It was my new barrel bank!

Not only were the design and authentic brown hue a significant improvement. But I didn't have to break it open, because it was plastic and reusable—I marveled at the ever-changing advancements of technology!

CHAPTER TWO

ONCE UPON A "SWITCH"

❦

So, right about now you're probably asking me via the literary continuum, "What does my piggy bank have to do with the price of the Louisiana Purchase?" Sorry—totally different historical reference, although that was a pretty smart deal.

Actually, something else important did happen to me when I was kid. I was introduced to the concept of banking another valuable cache, even though the process for obtaining it seemed more difficult and definitely much more painful.

Let me tell you another story. Once upon a time, when I was about eight or nine years old, for some reason I developed a very bad habit of leaving the house on Saturday mornings to hang out with my friends without letting my parents know.

They didn't know that I had left, nor where I had gone. I guess in my mind I had arrived at this new stage of juvenile independence and integrity—if words like that can ever be appropriately applied to someone that age. Basically, I began to assert authority I didn't have.

You see, after a few trial runs, my parents were pretty cool about me going out to play as long as they were kept in the loop. Back then it was a very different time, and I dare to say a lot safer. Parents in the neighborhood all knew each other and also knew each other's kids. The community connection made it easier for parents to keep track of our mutual friends who hung out together and associated with each other.

My older brother, Dehrric, also had a lot of friends in the neighborhood. But because he was seven years my senior, he obviously had much more autonomy to go out than me. He also bore the responsibility for looking out for me when we were out together.

My brother's friends were sort of my friends too, or so I wanted to think. But they were more like auxiliary older brothers who would help Dehrric with his chaperone duties, while benevolently playing along with me as I tagged along with him. Sometimes their choice of activities would change my status, requiring me to have to go back in the house.

I personally had three main friends whom I hung out with: my next-door neighbors Eddie, who was more my age, and his older brother, Maverick, and another good friend of mine from around the corner, Dwight. Eddie and I really didn't have a lot of momentous things to do. We just kind of palled around and ran and jumped in our adjacent backyards and the immediate neighborhood.

We amused ourselves by playing with whatever came to mind—trees, insects, rocks, kick balls, honeysuckles, childhood toys, games like tag, and the like. And yes, despite my God-given musical talents, which became my life's work later, I was still just a normal kid.

At least I was a normal kid some of the time, except when composing a small symphony or two! But as such there was nothing really unique or important about what Eddie and I did together—just regular boy stuff for our age.

Eddie and I both knew the rules with some minor differences between what my parents expected and what Eddie's allowed. We may have ventured close to the edge or even strayed a little across the red lines once or twice. But we both knew what awaited us if we totally disregarded the restrictions our parents had put in place for us.

So, let me pause here to convey that in those days, kids were a lot more respectful of parental rules than they seem to be now. Which is how we all (for the most part) made it out alive and lived to tell about it. I believe the sense of community relationships and neighborly support really helped to keep all us kids safe.

Even to this day I come across childhood friends who benefited greatly from those rules and connectedness. As a result, many are still alive and living in the same neighborhood where we all grew up. But I digress.

The flip side to all of this was that the older kids like my brother had a separate set of rules than the rest of us youngsters. They were members of that well-sought-after, post-parental-inquisition, self-governing "Well, he knows better" and "He's older than you" club.

Dehrric could go out to places and do cooler things than I could. His parting words to my parents when leaving out went something like, "Mom, I'll be back. I'm going around the corner." It was a much more assertive, "I'm in control of me" kind of vibe.

Incredibly my parents somehow were okay with that. Their response was, "Okay, Dehrric!" in this strangely cheerful, carefree tone of sorts. What in the world was that? I couldn't believe it! It really made me mad!

But after a while I figured it out. My parents were just allowing my brother to exercise some responsibility with a little freedom, while they still maintained a firm grip on the reins to pull him back whenever needed. I presumed that if I played my cards right, I'd eventually have that same kind of tempered privilege, too.

But as a simultaneous juxtaposition, when I tried something like that—to assert my young manhood and venture out—as soon as the jacket barely cleared the breadth of my shoulders, I got hit with all sorts of rapid-fire questions: "Where are you going?" "What's the address?" "Who are you going with?" "Will their parents be there?" "What's the telephone number?"

Then they followed-up with "Who else will be there with you?" "How long will you be out?" "What time will you be coming home?"

Next, they capped it all off with "Well, all right…don't you be late!" "Don't let me have to come get you!" Maybe some of you are familiar with this particular parental tone and drill.

Now bear in mind, this was just when I was going next door or right down the block! But also remember, there were no cell phones to speak of back then.

Fortunately, this maternal and paternal freak-out show didn't last too long on Broadway. But I think my parents were just instilling in me their concern and wanted me to be thoughtful and careful. Cool! I get it!

So, as they got more comfortable with me being responsible, I gradually grew more confident with pushing the limits of my outing entitlements, as well as collecting the benefits from my earned accreditation certificate for common sense. In other words, they started to let me imitate my brother's model of departure, just a little bit. They seemed to really accept that I would be obedient and trustworthy, if given the chance.

But you know what happened, right? I started blowing it. Remember what I said earlier about asserting authority I didn't have? Well, I started going out and hooking up with my friend Eddie on Saturday mornings to tour the neighborhood without letting my parents know anything. Again, remember: no cell phones.

So, you know when I got back home, I was greeted with that infamous "ARE YOU CRAZY, BOY!" stare of life-threatening disappointment. And maybe you know about that frozen-over glare that parents use to affix the entirety of their whole face upon yours for maximum eye contact? Well, that's what I got, too.

Nonetheless, I still got off with just a half-grin sneer, and a virtually sincere warning to me not to do it again. Not too bad. Cool!

But guess what? You know what I did? I did it again! And this time I stayed out all day! I really just wasn't thinking at all. So, when I finally got home my parents were absolutely livid!

They vacillated among several competing emotions of extreme worry and boiling anger, loving affection and deep disappointment. And their facial contortions looked like I'd be in trouble for at least the rest of my natural life if I lived, including adulthood!

Wow! I felt really, really bad. I can still feel that intense pressure in my chest and what felt like a heavy weight sitting on my head after all these years. I had never seen my parents react so strongly like that before.

And my parents were both what you would call "sweet" spirits. But regardless, they lowered the boom on me and grounded me from ever going out again, or until my twenty-first birthday, whichever one came later. Or possibly until they changed their minds.

I was so miserable and sad that I'd let down my parents, who believed in me and really trusted me. So, I was okay with being punished. I was. I really deserved it.

In fact, I actually committed to spending this newly found abundance of free time trying to think of ways to earn back their trust. So, I was just waiting for the right opportunity to show them—whenever that day would finally come—that I was a new man! Well, a new boy, technically.

Then miraculously that day did finally come! Ironically in a "Hitchcock" kind of twist, on a particular Saturday afternoon, it was my brother, Dehrric, this time who had gone rogue without any notice. He was gone so long that my parents really started to worry about him.

I heard all the commotion about it downstairs, but I stayed perfectly silent in my room as I soaked it all up—at least all that I could overhear. I eventually heard my dad say that he was going out to try to look for my brother.

But shortly after my dad left, this great big light bulb went on in my head! You see, my brother and I often went out and played together, as well. And we had our secret places where we liked to hang out.

So, the brilliant thought came to me: "I want to help! I know where my brother is. Our favorite spot, in the woods where we play in the leaves across the street!" This was my golden opportunity to restore my parents' faith and confidence in me! Yay!

At that very moment, I jumped to my feet, ran down the stairs, swung open the door, and ran out of the house at lightning speed across the street toward the woods. I was all excited to try to help find my brother, or at least be able to tell my father where I thought he might be.

As I entered the edge of the woods, after a little way in, I saw my father walking and heard him calling out to my brother, "Dehrric?" I got even more excited to help, and I was even a little worried about my brother, too.

But then all of the sudden this huge river of rushing memories and emotions started flooding my little mind with all kinds of eerie pulsations and terrifying feelings. "What was that?" I thought.

My warp speed began to robotically slow down to a virtual slow-motion stride, and then it all hit me. "What in the world am I doing?" I muttered.

"I just did the very thing I got punished for." It freaked me out so bad that I started sweating profusely while big fat tears started to well up in the corners of my eyes.

Then in my little brain I started to scheme. "Maybe if I just hide somewhere, my dad won't see me." So, what did I do? I found the nearest tree, plopped my little self down, and tried to conceal my body behind the trunk.

But I had a huge problem. The trunk of the tree was slightly smaller in width to that of my protruding torso, which by the way was sporting a bright blue, yellow, and white plaid shirt. I know, right?

Nevertheless, I sat very still, but all for naught. I didn't realize it at the time, but my father must have heard or seen me already because soon afterward I heard him change his call from "Dehrric" to "Terry…" He had this probing voice that sounded like sarcastic disbelief. "Is that you?"

Well, I had no choice now. I had to gather up some courage, stand up, turn around, come out from behind the tree, and face my father with this little tiny timid reply, "Yes, yes, Daddy."

I was scared, man. I was so terrified. But at the same time, I was so confused because with the best of intentions I had originally set out to do what I thought was a good thing (to help my dad search for my brother).

I just wanted to earn some of those trust points back. But I quickly realized that I had been disobedient in trying to do so. And as a last resort I attempted to explain it all away by telling my dad about where I thought Dehrric was.

Well, needless to say, as my dad approached me, he wasn't having it. And he wasn't open to any philosophical discussions about the matter. He yelled out, "Didn't I tell you not to come out the house without permission…didn't I!"

And yep, you got it—before I could barely get another two-word whimper out, he let me have it, right there in the woods. There was a virtual assortment of perfectly good switches to choose from, and one of them with my name on it was easily accessible to him in the nearby vicinity.

And as things got bad, all of the DC native birds and the other indigenous wildlife in the area jetted like crazy and scattered in every direction. And if my brother was anywhere near to be found, he was long gone by now.

After it was all over, Dad yelled again and told me to go home and wait for him there. I started running back to the house as fast as I could with tears streaming down my face, while my rear end and humbled pride stung like I had never felt before.

Dearly beloved, that was the very first day of my life—the very moment that I began the process of obtaining, amassing, and banking what I later came to know as "wisdom." In the Bible, Proverbs 13:1 (NIV) says it best: "A wise son heeds his father's instruction, but a mocker does not respond to rebukes."

Now, let me take a short *Selah* here. I know there are some people who believe no form of punishment that involves spanking a child should ever be used or allowed. But in those days in our African American culture, spanking was not only common, but widely encouraged, even biblically.

Proverbs 13:24 (NLT) says, "Those who spare the rod of discipline hate their children. Those who love their children care enough to discipline them."

Even so, my father hadn't really spanked me that hard. I think him having to do so hurt him even more than me. In fact, I was hurting mostly from having disobeyed him and seeing the disappointment in his eyes. The pain from the spanking was less important.

But the pain, as much or as little as it was, was severe enough to drive the point home. Looking back, I'm so grateful that my dad loved me enough to discipline me when I needed it, just as the Bible instructs.

I also learned some very important—and, I might add, painful—principles that day. And I learned even more in the days that followed. They stuck with me and established a firm foundation for my journey forward through life.

I learned about fear, obedience, pain, trust, love, respect, and a few other things. They have all helped to guide my development and understanding over the years.

And it puts a finer point on another scripture I learned. Proverbs 22:6 (NKJV) says, "Train up a child in the way he should go: and when he is old, he will not depart from it."

I definitely learned things that I never forgot that helped to guide my future decisions. And as a side note, I never got another spanking again. That was my very last one, praise God!

But something else even deeper and more important began to grow up in me and grow me up, from those early childhood days to now. My parents were my introduction not only to God leading to a personal relationship with the Lord, Jesus Christ, but also an inclination and a thirst to pursue, obtain, and understand the bountiful treasures of wisdom.

CHAPTER THREE

THE REAL FEAR FACTOR

∼

I'M NOT SURE IF MANY people remember the hit show *Fear Factor* from the early 2000s (2001–2006, to be exact). *Fear Factor* was a game show based on the premise of pitting contestants against each other to complete a variety of scary and sometimes disgusting stunts, to ultimately win a grand prize of $50,000.

This show was quite popular for a while, and I even watched a few episodes myself. But I came away from my viewing experience asking the question, "Why would anyone put themselves through all of that just to win some money, even as much as $50,000?"

I concluded that I would never do anything like that. Maybe I was speaking from a place of pride, or self-respect, or maybe just fear. But that kind of fear on the screen as portrayed is not true fear.

First of all, it was a game show on television. That tells you pretty much everything. The point of the show was to excite the TV viewing audience as much as possible. As the contestants faced off and demonstrated their alleged fear, the payoff for the show was to generate the highest degree of empathic fear for the audience

This heightened reaction from thrill-seeking viewers would then hopefully compel them to come back every week and watch it over and over again. Thus, high ratings and big sponsor dollars.

But as TV viewers, we can't see everything that's going on behind the scenes. This includes all the preparations and safeguards put in place. We may have also found that what we were seeing with our eyes wasn't actually happening at all. It could have been proven to be bogus or at best, misleading. And many times, shows like this were found to be so.

However, there is "real life." Real life presents authentic experiences and obstacles that aren't stunts. And true fear is not something that people consider exciting, at least not in a positive way.

In addition, there's an aspect of fear that people may not normally experience or understand whatsoever. This fear is even more serious than that presented on a game show, or during times when they're genuinely scared. This deeper sense of fear can become more significant to us on a personal level in dealing with the multilayered challenge of living.

In the Bible, Psalm 111:10 (NLT) explains that, "Fear of the Lord is the foundation of true wisdom. All who obey his commandments will grow in wisdom. Praise him forever!" So, when I learned about fear as a child, it progressively took me through several stages of profound understanding.

First, fear in its most basic state represents an innate response to what is perceived as unfamiliar, uncomfortable, unpleasant, or mysterious. Or it's something human nature observes or interprets as potentially harmful or dangerous.

Fear causes us to instinctively recoil or even flee from whatever it is that triggers our reaction. In fact, there are chemical reactions within the human body and the brain at work. But the bottom line is that a natural, built-in response occurs, which helps us to protect our survival as human beings.

We also need training and education from parents, family members, teachers, friends, and others who have already lived life long enough to experience painful and fear-bearing situations. They warn us as a preemptive measure about potential dangers and help us to reasonably avoid new encounters similar to those they endured or to which they were exposed.

These warnings can be in the form of full-fledged sermons, speeches, or discussions—that is, if we're mature enough at the time to receive and understand information on that level. But even from a small child's perspective, it may be as simple as assertive body language, like a sudden gesture of the hand or an unpleasant facial expression. Or it could be a sharp, loud tone of the voice, or even an abrupt yell or scream saying, "Stop!"

The child might not totally comprehend the words you're saying, but they will certainly get the message and remember the feeling they felt from the warning. So, the next time they feel that same way, they'll instinctively seek escape to avoid a similar warning or the potential danger itself.

But sometimes the only way for a child to understand the significance of fear is to go through situations in which they actually experience some level of tangible pain. Again, remember Proverbs 13:24. Even the first pain a child recognizes may be at childbirth, when the doctor or nurse physically promotes the process of breathing, normally causing the baby to cry.

Pain immediately impacts the human consciousness in a way that permanently imprints that corresponding tangible source of fear. And it automatically trains us to circumvent whatever that thing is that may physically harm us. For instance, kids are curiously attracted to bright shiny objects and lights—things such as fire. But if they ever stick their hand out and get burned, even slightly, their newfound fear of fire will help them to avoid experiencing that pain and a more severe injury in the future. In other words, they develop a kind of "respect" for the fire and what it can do. And they learn to obey their internalized warning and not go beyond a perceived boundary that would result in pain.

This can also translate into the fear of emotional, mental, and spiritual pain as we gradually mature into adulthood. But generally speaking, physical pain jump-starts the entire process of understanding the warning signs that fear evokes, and it will ultimately lead to addressing the more complex fear responses associated with the aforementioned introspective types of pain.

Secondly, fear has a flip side. When I disobeyed my dad on that Saturday afternoon, it took me a while to really understand what I did wrong. I wasn't fully aware of the extent of what was going on.

Both my dad and also my grandmother, who was living with us at the time, explained it all to me later. But in fact, I really didn't fully appreciate it until I had children of my own. But that's a completely different story and probably worth another book that I may just write.

However, even way before that full-blown epiphany as an adult, I learned that the fear I felt regarding my dad was a surface response to the temporary pain he introduced to me. It was intended to teach me right from wrong. And I knew that my dad loved me, as demonstrated by his consistent affection and provisions for me. So, what in fact was going on?

I started to understand something much deeper. My father and my mother were responsible for me: my well-being, my safety, my food, my clothing, my shelter, my education, my everything.

As a child all I knew for the most part was Mom and Dad. And they readily provided all that I needed, including a strong nurturing environment and an affectionate family structure. So, again why would my dad want me to experience pain? What was the point?

Well, I gradually began to recognize that my dad wanted to keep me from going through an even greater level of pain in my life. I needed to learn to fear the risk of a greater pain, which would bring even more severe consequences.

I had to learn to pay attention and, moreover, proactively look for the warning signs myself to avoid danger and harm. But in the meantime, I needed to trust and obey my parents during this crucial learning period.

For instance, if I were to have disobeyed my parents by leaving out the house again and not tell them, they may not have been able to be there to protect me if something went wrong or threatened my safety. So, my dad was teaching me to respect his role as my father enough to learn the value of his counsel based upon those vital lessons he shared from his own experiences. These lessons would then help me later to seek safety and keep an eye out for danger even when he wasn't around.

Thirdly, my parents were extremely wise people. Why? Because they in fact had lived and had studied life for a long time. They were well aware of things I had no earthly idea existed.

My parents knew of and sheltered me from the evil lurking in the world. And they protected me from the perverted ills of what some people are capable of doing.

So, the fear I experienced was a drop in the bucket compared to the level of fear they would have felt, and the pain they would have experienced, if I had gotten kidnapped or shot or something worse—too terrible to imagine. I needed to be considerate of their feelings, too.

Finally, Proverbs 1:7 (NIV) declares, "The fear of the LORD is the beginning of knowledge, but fools despise wisdom and instruction." Being a fool was never something I ever wanted to appear on my future resume. So, this lesson of fear was most important as it referred to the supreme respect and reverence for God.

My father's loving discipline that I received through temporary pain provided a model for me of what God is like, and what it means to fear or respect him—a God that I would later come to know personally through the knowledge of his son, the Lord, Jesus Christ. I would eventually learn about the wise acceptance of his grace, as revealed and made possible through his sacrifice for me. This was that deeper sense of fear or reverence that leads to accessing the most precious treasures of God's wisdom.

CHAPTER FOUR

LOOKING FORWARD—THE MAGNITUDE OF WISDOM

I WANTED TO PAUSE HERE for a moment to take note of where we are in this discussion, and where we're going. The enormity of this moment really needs to be emphasized. We're dealing with some serious life-altering, major-league stuff here—pardon my use of such extremely technical terminology.

But for many people, achieving the status of truly being wise is a lofty, white-collar-like, even "boushy" type of vibe. This mindset exists regardless of the fact that many successful people from a human perspective boast about wisdom, and the wise decisions and strategies they used are at the root of what they have accomplished. In their minds this sets them apart and provides the reason why they are where they are in the food chain.

But the magnitude of true wisdom goes far beyond the reach of human aspirations. It brings the discussion to a level that transcends the human attitude toward natural law (as depicted by Greek and Roman philosophers). (Note: Not to get too deep in the weeds, the Wikipedia article "Natural Law" says, "Natural law refers to the use of reason to analyze human nature in deducing binding rules of moral behavior.")

Nevertheless, let me back up and begin from where I left off. How can anyone be a recipient of any gift from God, including grace, unless they deal realistically with God on his terms as the creator? How can they be a beneficiary of God's favor without fearing and/or respecting him enough to believe and trust him, esteem him, obey him, and do what he says?

Ironically, we know that God cares for us, based upon the significance of his continual provisions for us, which demonstrate that he already and has always had our best interest at heart. This is true even though often it involves painful experiences—which ultimately teach us about something more valuable and precious as seen through God's eyes.

By observing biblical history, we see that Christians from the very beginning went through and endured so much physical pain for the cause of Christ. Jesus's apostles and disciples suffered greatly, even unto death, for their devotion to Christ. They remained committed to his teachings of salvific faith and to their commissioned calling.

Why would they do this for something not proven or understood to be of true value—riches far beyond what could be obtained in this world? And Jesus himself bore the most pain ever known to mankind for the purpose of completing God's salvation plan for all humanity, for what?

What was at the center of all this pain poured out for each of us? It had to have been for something greater than even we could reasonably grasp or comprehend on a human scale. Was it about God's supernatural wisdom and power expressed through love?

Was it the outpouring of true love, which requires a confrontation with pain and its intrinsic fear or respect for God, that would nurture obedience to him? Or maybe this pain is not only for those who believe and follow Jesus, but pain that has to be experienced by God, himself?

Going back to Psalm 111:10, "Fear of the Lord is the foundation of true wisdom. All who obey his commandments and teachings will grow in wisdom..." So, the fear of the Lord or respect and reverence for him engenders a posture of commitment to do what God says to do—the same as with the example of Jesus Christ himself.

That's the basis for obtaining and administering the powerful feats and outcomes of wisdom. This is true wisdom—a wisdom that is always valid and always works.

This is "spiritual wisdom" born out of sacrifice. And it draws upon the eternal bank account of supernatural treasure, the guarantor of whom is God himself.

Humble obedience to God will produce a life that is successful and effective, because of the wise counsel, informed choices, sound decisions, and trusted actions taken based upon spiritual wisdom. And it can only be found in God. Therefore, because it is of God, it can never fail, not even throughout time or eternity.

CHAPTER FIVE
THE PARADOX OF FEAR

So, you may be pondering how fear can be triggered in response to pain, ultimately resulting in profound respect, reverence, and obedience, while also existing as a fear that promotes feelings of just "being afraid" of an imminent threat or danger, causing a prioritization to preserve or protect one's own safety.

But then there's the wildcard of fear, based on a feeling of apprehension that sparks hesitancy in making decisions, or a kneejerk reaction to make foolish ones devoid of any wisdom-based considerations. How do these three applications or versions of fear work separately or possibly interrelate? And how might they be relevant, if at all?

Since we're on the path of pursuing spiritual wisdom as it relates to fear, we're faced with what appears to be a contradiction or paradox. Do you remember what I explained earlier about the fearing or being afraid of my dad—as not the kind of fear that ultimately leads to true wisdom?

Rather, it is respect or reverence that's the type of fear that allows us to learn about wisdom. We learn through our parents, through other mentors, and finally from God directly to gain insight into wisdom's full range of spiritual power.

On every level God's wisdom is greatly superior to that of human understanding. Human wisdom, in and of itself, disproportionately relies on the emotions of being frightened, and anxious in the moment as guiding principles for many major life decisions and actions.

Some of these decisions can be completely at odds with the nature of true wisdom and the scope of what is achievable through it. For instance, actions just based on "being afraid" can become rooted in human selfishness, envy, or evil intent. They work to carry out dangerous impulses, acquire material gain, and fulfill other types of transient benefits. These narrow-minded gains and profits conform to a human-centered worldview and abased standard of living.

But on the other hand, there's this kind of fear or fright-based wisdom that can cause people to lack the motivation they need to act in a positive and productive manner. They fear failure, lack self-esteem, and are devoid of the courage needed to move forward, do good, and fight for what is right. They are more interested in trying to simply protect themselves from experiencing any hurt or danger, or criticism for that matter.

Herein lies the apparent paradox. How can being afraid be advantageous in moving us as a child, as an adult, or as a people toward understanding the reverence of God, and thereby his wisdom? And then simultaneously be the kind of fear that can move us away from God's purpose, to then pursue negative motivations and selfish goals?

Well, we can find at least some of the answers in

2 Timothy 1:7 (ESV), which says, "For God gave us a spirit not of fear but of power and love and self-control." Also, Bible Study Tools explains that in this scripture passage, "fear" is translated from "the word in the Greek [which] is deilia (di-lee-ah). This word means cowardice or timidity. A person with a spirit of fear or timidity may shy away from proclaiming the gospel or upholding the truth of God's Word. This happens because of an impending sense of threat or danger whether it is real or imagined."

Therefore, this kind of fear is not suitable on any human level, nor on any spiritual level. If someone is frightened to the point of not being able to act or move, they won't be able to take advantage of the power that true wisdom wheels and all that it can accomplish.

But remember that 2 Timothy 1:7 is affirming that God has not given us the spirit of fear or cowardice. So, in fact, it affirms that God "has" given us the spirit of power, and love, and self-control—which is the spiritual fruit produced from a life committed to God, and also the divine treasures his wisdom affords.

CHAPTER SIX

TRANSITIONING FROM FEAR TO WISDOM'S POWER

So, what allows us to apprehend this "spirit of power, and love, and self-control"? As we've seen, the concept of "fear" from a human point of view is somewhat complex. It conjures up all kinds of emotions and various applications in diverse circumstances.

But we have to adopt a much more mature approach while maneuvering within our mission in life. We have to advance from fear to the superior power and treasures of God's wisdom.

True wisdom brings to the table a variety of strengths and a sense of stability that fear can't. Just like an apprenticeship, fear serves to teach us the way and direct us toward wisdom's power. And once there, we'll have no incentive or reason to regress.

Once fear teaches us what our life is like in the physical world as its dangers and threats lurk in the darkness all around us, and then we apprehend the knowledge and practice of not being afraid, we're now at the point of taking our experiences to the next stage by respecting God and embracing his guidance.

We can now graduate to true wisdom, which dwells in the perfect light of God's love, truth, and understanding. We can't continue to function on human terms, but on a spiritual level at which the power of wisdom influences both the choices and decisions we make for ourselves, and also perfects the aspirations we have for the success and goodwill of others through Jesus Christ.

First Corinthians 2:1–5 (NKJV) explains the process of this transition very well by stating,

And I, brethren, when I came to you, did not come with excellence of speech or of wisdom declaring to you the testimony (*mystery*) of God. For I determined not to know anything among you except Jesus Christ and Him crucified.

I was with you in weakness, in fear, and in much trembling. And my speech and my preaching *were* not with persuasive words of (*human*) wisdom, but in demonstration of the Spirit and of power, that your faith should not be in the wisdom of men but in the power of God.

For a personal example, there were some pivotal moments in my life when my understanding on a human level simply proved inadequate for all that I was going through. And as I describe later in chapter 14, there are choices you just have to make when it's the right thing to do. It's difficult, but you still have to make the decision.

So, as my little story goes, I eventually did grow up from my childhood somewhat, although there are a whole host of other stories I could share—and probably will—from that seriously intense edification period of my humble existence.

But during my initial high school days, I experienced some fairly radically new things, to put it mildly. This was that predestined point at which my Christian upbringing came into the greatest conflict and sharpest contrasts with my budding social network and internal impulses.

So, I think you can guess what I mean…and of course as I shared before, I was a thriving young musician from an early age. And, by now I was considered somewhat of a local "star," and a so-called "prodigy." I had already been performing on the national stage and television, primarily in Christian circles.

But just so you know, this kind of characterization didn't really mean a whole lot to me at the time, mainly because that wasn't the vernacular used much in the environment in which I was raised. But I did begin to take notice of all the attention I was getting.

And being a musician has always gotten me loads of attention, especially during that time when "the look" was all about Michael Jackson and his iconic "bush" hairstyle. It was "all the craze"—of which I had one of the biggest ever known to man.

I still blush when I see the pictures. And it's funny how former classmates I've met up with later from that era still seem to just remember that about me. They say things like, "Yeah, I remember you and that big bush, man!"

But, needless to say, from the first day I stepped across the threshold of my new high school's entranceway I became quite popular. It wasn't necessarily my goal, but it just happened.

And now that I think of it, I actually had a lot of previous experience from my junior high school days to reflect upon—both as a young musician playing in a band, and also with being popular. But high school was a completely different animal. New school, new friends, new interests, and yes, new girls that sparked my immediate attention in a huge way.

So, the thing was that even though I was brought up in a Christian home, a home environment with strong Christian values and principles that everyone followed, and even though I was fortunate to be blessed with both parents and my family praying for me constantly, I wasn't actually a Christian yet. I hadn't personally accepted Jesus Christ into my life.

I knew who Jesus was, at least in my head. I acted like a Christian outwardly. And I had a real desire to do what was right because of how I was raised. But I hadn't taken that last step—that vitally important step of personally accepting the gift of salvation and eternal life into my heart. I was still flying under the radar on the spiritual coattails of my parents and my family.

That was cool when I was younger. But now I was at the age when I needed to face my own personal mortality, morality, and responsibility for my own actions and choices.

I now had to try to navigate this brand-new culture, freedom, and terrain in which I was abruptly dropped. And, I had to do this while persistently hearing all those stern voices and warnings in my mind telling me what I should and shouldn't do, and the things I needed to avoid. (Note: Don't forget what I shared in the second chapter. You can do a quick review, if needed. I'll wait…)

So, as this new culture began to rub off on me, some of those internal messages started to take a back seat to the experiences and sensations I was feeling. Yet I was still feeling the conflict, and I continued to hear those voices. It was both scary and oddly exciting. Wow, dude! Human liberation meets spiritual restraints!

Fortunately, before I got too far out on the limb and out of my mind, I had some former folks and some new friends my age in my corner. They became a strong influence and anchor in my life from a Christian perspective.

I wasn't out there swimming in this big ocean of swarming temptations and raging waves all by my lonesome. God just does stuff like that! It's not only because of the prayers of the saints, but also because he has his own reasons and planned agenda in mind to keep you close and safe.

Concurrently, I had been attending church and youth Bible study. And at some point, one of my great friends, Ronald, witnessed to me one evening on the way home. He really broke things down for me. Ronald was extremely smart and articulate for his age.

But there was this one issue riding in the background of my brain—at least one doctrinal point of confusion. I had this unresolved issue from a while back that made it more difficult for me to fully understand what I needed to do.

It was a real stumbling block for me. Nonetheless, I had to do something or I was going to slowly slip into the deep end and drown! My human understanding even in terms of what I knew and comprehended about Jesus just wasn't working.

So, my friend explained it all to me, and finally I was sold, both spiritually and intellectually. And now I was at peace with my decision to give my life to Jesus Christ.

And, no…there wasn't any burning bush with golden embers soaring across the sky and raining down from the vast realms of the heavens. And the ground didn't crumble and open up into a swallowing sea of lava, as the fields and the trees melted like wax into the immense earthquake valleys, with tremors rumbling all around me.

For that matter, I didn't even experience an out-of-body, transcendental epiphany, which apparently some people do. But what I did have was this sweet assurance and heart-soothing peace with a new understanding of who I was and who I now became in Christ.

My parents and my family had planted all the right seeds and watered me daily with their knowledge and example of the great wisdom of the Lord. They gave me the right footing on the right foundation on which to stand. And they fed me with the nurturing Word of God—even if I wasn't totally clear on what it all meant for me personally.

But I finally made that crucial step to move away from the fear of consequences and confusion. I shifted from a surface respect for God, to a personal choice and decision to sincerely follow Jesus. And finally, I turned away from living my life according to my own human way of thinking and coping, to a new life perspective in God's wisdom and direction.

But again, let me be clear: Although my transition from an experiential fear to a wisdom-based faith truly occurred, it was still going to be a lifelong process of growth and maturation. I would still need to travel down a road peppered with both triumphs and failures for all the years that were to follow. But at least this time I was on my own path and walking with God for myself.

I was then, and am now, able to experience for myself the amazing treasure of God's wisdom that my parents knew for themselves based upon their personal walk with the Lord. And as a generational legacy, they have now transitioned this "spirit of power, and love, and self-control" to me! Accepting Jesus as my personal Savior and Lord was the wisest decision I ever made, and it will always be…

CHAPTER SEVEN

ASSESSING AGELESS WISDOM VERSUS CONTEMPORARY UNDERSTANDING

※

Now going back to the premise of *Wisdom Treasures*, it's very important to recognize the ageless quality of godly wisdom versus the finite and fleeting personality of what people today exalt as true enlightenment and understanding. One phenomenon that happens on a fairly regular basis is the incessant revision and frankly embarrassing modification of what acclaimed scholars and the world's leading authorities testify to as being unmitigated wisdom and truth.

These revisions are more likely than not to be made in the darkness of night—when most people aren't paying much attention, rather than in the light of transparency. They just kind of show up on the world's stage. And everyone is supposed to accept them without question because of the celebrated source or resource from which they come.

But sometimes changes are made boldly and presented as brilliant new discoveries—inspired revelations that have easily eluded all of the rest of us morons and average thinkers—when the fact is, these acclaimed authorities were just wrong about their prior assertions and don't want to admit it.

It's obvious that most people, no matter how smart and experienced they are, don't like to be wrong about anything. Even the smallest detail is too much to stomach. Unfortunately, this is true about most people. And it's probably true about you and me.

But let me clarify something. It doesn't mean that we actually declare aloud that we're right all the time, although some people really do that.

However, it does mean that the burning feeling inside or that inclining pressure of pride rises up in us whenever what we say or believe is challenged. It's a very human quality and a very typical human response.

I'm not quite sure when pride starts to show up in our human DNA or development. But I know it has to start quite early. Or maybe it really is just a part of who we are when we're born.

And most likely it's unwittingly nurtured within us as children during the formative years, when we think all we have to do is frown or cry or throw a tantrum and we can get just about whatever we want. And then, somehow that causes us to selfishly believe we're always right about everything we want, based on what we understand.

I know that's somewhat speculative on my part. But at any rate, I do think that believing you're always right is an immature human trait. And when it's full-blown in adults, it can cause some serious issues in our lives. If we don't rein it in early and learn to control it, far more dire consequences await us.

But one amazing thing God does for us is to reveal who we are as human beings. He does this so we can become much more with him than we could ever become or accomplish on our own.

In other words, God makes us understand the limitations of our abilities (as human beings)—the confines within our own strength and knowledge—so that he can empower within us all that we're capable of doing in him, through Jesus Christ. I know that sounds a little intricate, but it really isn't.

Let's take a very simple example of mine. When I was around the age of sixteen or seventeen, I learned to drive from my father. And although my dad was a very even-tempered, patient person in general, I never wanted to do anything to make him angry, because I loved him.

And I honestly didn't want to land myself in any trouble. But that wasn't even the issue. Still, I was quite intimidated by the idea of learning to drive from my father, at least when we first started.

The main thing was that my dad owned this huge midnight-blue Mercury Marquis in pristine spanking condition. It was shiny like a mirror on the outside and immaculate on the inside. And it smelled so nice, because he washed it often at the carwash.

He got those little evergreen tree air fresheners, which he hung from the rearview mirror that made it smell like Christmastime all year round. And the ride was so smooth that sometimes it felt like we were gliding across the road on glass.

So, when he suggested that we use his car to teach me how to drive, I said, "What?" "Me?" "Really?" He calmly but optimistically responded, "Yeah, sure."

I couldn't believe it. Me behind that wheel? In all that car? All I could think of was me driving along and then gliding right off that glass of a road into a big tree or a ditch! I couldn't even imagine what his reaction might be if I wrecked his car.

But my dad just had this cool way about him. He knew I was nervous and in his own calm demeanor he explained everything to me about the car and the controls.

He made sure that I understood everything. And then he lovingly reassured me that everything would be okay. He told me not to worry because he would be right there with me in case anything happened.

So, the more he talked with me and set my mind at ease, I began to look forward to my driving lessons with him. My dad was a great driver, and he was also very methodical. So, in those days passing the driving road test included a little something called "parallel parking."

Now, let me take just a moment to vent here—gently, of course. Parking for some strange reason has now been officially deleted from several state road tests. I don't know why, and I don't know what wise gurus decided to make this happen.

I truly don't understand. Maybe it was some masterminded conspiratorial kickback plot involving the DMV and the car manufacturing companies, already working on their future self-parking technology and rear-view backup systems for the new crop of twenty-first-century vehicles.

I don't know. But let me strongly declare to you, this was not well thought out at all. Why? Because of all the young drivers beginning their new driving experiences in the world in between the previous era and currently, as well as those who don't own cars with the newfangled self-parking features. *They don't know how to park!* Sorry…I'm not trying to be mean here.

But some drivers take all day and forever trying to maneuver into a space where a curb is involved. And if they have to park on the left side of a one-way street, you will be in for a very long, long wait.

In fact, one day I happened to be dining at one of my favorite restaurants that has a lot of windows. All of the patrons, including me, were relaxed and enjoying our meals, when all of the sudden I noticed the eyes and heads of those around me starting to trend in the direction of the window closest to me. Then they all locked their necks in position and began to stare.

So, I naturally began to follow the crowd and turn my head to look, too. I thought maybe an accident had occurred, or maybe a beautiful newlywed couple was on the way to grace our presence for a reception upstairs, which actually does happen occasionally there. But, no—it wasn't any of those things.

It happened to be a lady trying to parallel park her car manually. She desperately tried, and she tried, and she tried, backing up and turning, and going forward again, and turning again.

I cringed as I looked on with everyone else—as she moved dangerously close to hitting the other vehicles in front and in back of her. Unfortunately, nothing was going right for her. She sadly was just not able do it.

Finally, she gave up, and the passenger in her car sheepishly got out and proceeded to park the car for her—as the original driver looked on in embarrassment. This was really kind of sad, and I really felt bad for her.

But I have a public service announcement and a word of wisdom for everyone today. Everyone—PLEASE LEARN HOW TO PARALLEL PARK!

It doesn't matter if it's not required on your road test. It doesn't even matter if you have one of those new twenty-first-century cars that can self-park. Learn how to manually park a car anyway.

Why? Because you never know if your new car will ever malfunction, which does occur quite often these days. Computers do crash (please pardon the pun). Or you may have to drive another car at some point that doesn't have the self-parking feature.

Believe me, if you learn to park, you'll thank me later. By the way, teach your children how to park, too. They will also thank me later. And maybe you, too.

Just remember, technology, no matter how well intended, makes our brains take little tiny unscheduled vacations every once in a while. It makes us just a little dumb about the most common things that we're normally very competent to do for ourselves. But that's simply where we are now...

Okay, now that I've offered my very small piece of wisdom-based counsel, hopefully to someone out there who needed it, I trust that I've done my civic duty for today. And I do pray that I wasn't too mean about it. But I felt that I really needed to be honest and just get that out there in the culture for the greater good.

Okay...Now, let's get back to my story. As I was saying, with my dad being the methodical person he was, the very first thing he did was to take me outside to the car to teach me how to parallel park.

I was relieved and okay with that, because I thought, "Wow, going five miles an hour, how much damage could I possibly do?" Of course, having to go in reverse hadn't quite crossed the full scope of my imagination.

While wanting to keep things realistic for me, Dad also wanted to maintain the safety of other cars on the street. So, he devised this idea to use mic stands (as a musical family, we obviously had several) to mark the parameters of a parking space for me to use to learn how to park.

Our street during those days was pretty quiet with very little traffic. Of course, that has changed a lot over the years.

But my dad's strategy worked! I learned probably the most difficult part of the road test first. And then he proceeded to take me out to learn how to actually drive the car. I was fully acquainted with all mirrors, dashboard displays, and the operational controls of the car, mainly because of all the parking lessons.

So, then we went out to drive on large vacant parking lots and neighborhood streets with minimal traffic. While we drove, Dad reviewed the traffic rules I had learned during the written test.

Then as I demonstrated more skill and confidence, he took me onto some pretty busy city streets, and then finally onto the highway. One thing he would always do when we returned home was to make me park the car again by myself.

Dad's patience, calm demeanor, and words of praise and encouragement during our rides really helped me to feel at ease. It diffused any prior fear I may have had.

So, by the time the day came for my actual road test, I felt very relaxed and ready, even in this great big huge car of his. But the car actually didn't feel so big anymore, now that I knew everything about how to operate it.

I admit I was still a little nervous because now there was someone I didn't know in the car with me, grading me on every little move I made during my now "official" driving performance test. But Dad had prepared me thoroughly, and I passed the test the very first time with flying colors.

I particularly aced the parking portion of the test like a pro! Dad was very proud of me, and we celebrated afterward!

Now, years later when I drive, wherever I go I don't have to think any more about any of the individual steps or the lessons we had back then. No matter how old I get, I just drive like it's an automatic function of my mind and my body. My understanding of driving and the car have become an involuntary extension of myself on the road.

Apart from an intermittent backseat driving experience with my lovely wife in the front seat, I'm usually completely confident and in control of what I'm doing and where I'm going. Yet technology strikes again by making me feel lost occasionally if I don't use my GPS when driving to unfamiliar places—and even some that are familiar.

So, what's the moral of this story? As I said before, God teaches us to understand the limitations of our abilities, which occur within our own strength and knowledge (as human beings). This is so he can become in us all that we're capable of doing in him, through Jesus Christ.

When my dad taught me how to drive, in his wisdom he addressed my limitations and fears head-on, first by slowly familiarizing me with all that I didn't know, using all that was at my disposal to use. Then he taught me the experience and process of learning to operate in a mature realm of understanding, while he was there to protect me if something went wrong.

Finally, with the experience of going through a test and passing it, I was ready to operate based on the knowledge and understanding I had acquired, which became integrated into who I was and all I would be in the future.

This kind of maturity allows us to operate on a level of understanding that instinctively utilizes the wisdom obtained from and through the teachings of our parents and ultimately God, even from long ago. We're then able to humbly address the condition of those who may choose to remain in the immature wisdom of this current earthly realm, and convincingly offer them a better path.

Our wisdom from God is like a mystery that transcends human ego, pride, understanding, and existence. And thereby we're brought into the very hope God has orchestrated throughout the ages, which is to reveal his definitive plan through Jesus Christ. That hope and plan can't be known or understood through mere human intellect or impetuous motivations.

First Corinthians 2:6–9 (NIV) speaks to this by stating,

> We do, however, speak a message of wisdom among the mature, but not the wisdom of this age or of the rulers of this age, who are coming to nothing. No, we declare God's wisdom, a mystery that has been hidden and that God destined for our glory before time began.
>
> None of the rulers of this age understood it, for if they had, they would not have crucified the Lord of glory. However, as it is written: "What no eye has seen, what no ear has heard, and what no human mind has conceived" [Isaiah 64:4]—the things God has prepared for those who love him.

Therefore, it's evident that God's wisdom exists on a level of maturity far beyond the natural capability of human beings to obtain, understand, and process in any practical sense. Insight derived from human life experiences and their situational application cannot be authenticated as examples of God's wisdom—unless God himself chooses to reveal that understanding to us spiritually. And the essence of that revelation of God's wisdom is fully embodied in the person of Jesus Christ, who was rejected by those lacking the spiritual insight to recognize who and what he was and is.

CHAPTER EIGHT
GOD'S REVELATION OF SPIRITUAL WISDOM

So then, the question remains that if God's desire and intent is for us to both seek and obtain his wisdom, and it can only be achieved through his proactive spiritual revelation—in other words, God's choice to cause it to occur—then what is God's method or vehicle by which this revelation can be delivered and received?

I have learned over my life that God does what he does, the way he does it for a specific reason and purpose. God isn't just randomly throwing around decisions to see what will stick to the wall when he's done.

He has a plan and a strategy to accomplish all that his word and his will have set into motion. This is the case on a macro, mezzo, and micro level.

When I was growing up, and for the major part of my early adult life, my paternal and maternal grandmothers were both very prominent in my world. They were the matriarchs of our family from whom much of our relational and cultural understanding flowed.

In their presence and interaction with us, they always imparted this deep sense of belonging and connection with our roots. They embodied our history and instilled our modern social value and purpose in all the members of our family.

Being born into this amazing quilt of individuals, finely woven together, provided a warm, comforting environment of love. It somehow spiritually reached far beyond any limitations of physical distance or interpersonal conflict or barriers.

We could and did all come together under the nurturing wings of Mama and Grandma, respectively. And we experienced and learned to understand the power that our family's arc of safety, acceptance, and inclusion created and provided.

So, remember what I said about God not doing anything without a specific and intentional purpose? Well, interestingly enough, my paternal grandmother's first name was Ellen, and my maternal grandmother's first name was Ella.

It's no coincidence that both the name Ellen and Ella come from the English and Greek meaning "light," "torch," or "bright," or "bright, shining light." Ella also means "God with us" and from the German origin means "entire" or "all, completely." Ella also means "other" or "further/additional" or "a person or thing that is distinct or different from that already known about."

They both were very spiritually enlightened and served to guide our family into the realm of practical and godly understanding. Grandma (Ellen) seemed to fulfill the role of imparting a sweet light of nurturing counsel and God-worshipping, God-fearing, righteous living wisdom. While Mama (Ella) fulfilled a role of exposing us to an everyday functional, resolute purpose and a self-sacrificial, compassionate, love-in-action wisdom.

One very special memory I have of Grandma (Ellen) was her unobstructed reverence for God. I always saw her praying and reading her Bible every day. And in everything, she gave thanks and constantly worshipped and praised God.

Even as Grandma got older and her health began to fail, she always mustered up whatever strength she could and openly testified about the goodness of the Lord. And I know many of those times, God was bearing witness through her of himself to us.

But most of the time she was talking directly to God. She didn't mind letting out a heartfelt "Hallelujah!" or "Thank you, Jesus!" no matter who was around.

She was just an authentic, uniquely faithful, sweet spirit in the Lord. And she was a very strong believer who consistently expressed her trust in and dependence upon God.

Grandma also had this way of making sure my brother and I respected God. She didn't take any foolishness from either one of us when it came to being reverent, thankful, and obedient.

I especially remember the times when thunderstorms would come. As soon as Grandma noticed the darkened clouds, or a single flash of lightning, or even a firm sway of the trees, she'd immediately shut the windows, close the curtains, and have us cut the TV off.

If anybody happened to be on the phone, you had to get off, right away. And then we had to cut off all the lights, sit down, and be quiet. We couldn't even talk. Then we just sat there, still, and waited until the storm passed over.

That was just Grandma's way. And the whole family respected and followed her example and her instructions. I didn't fully understand it then when I was young.

But I realized later that she was showing her fear or respect for God's sovereignty and power. She used to say when the storm came up, "That's God working" or "speaking." Then she'd say, "Be quiet now, and let him speak..."

On the other hand, when it came to my other grandmother, Mama (Ella), she was the one who always loved bringing the whole family together on all the holidays and on other special occasions. We often gathered at her house for these great big, amazing dinners she cooked.

And during summer vacations, we went down to her beach house to stay weekends, or longer if we were able to. We absolutely loved the long station wagon rides, the games, the big breakfasts, and especially the swimming pool.

Mama really loved seeing the family, especially all the kids together having a good time. And she really loved doing things that made us all happy. Mama was such a wise, loving, giving, and generous spirit, to the point that she adopted several disadvantaged kids (girls) over the years and taught and raised them as her own.

But one thing Mama absolutely insisted on was us all doing what was right, doing our part when it came to chores, and learning to work hard to keep things nice. She stressed that it was great having nice things, but we should appreciate them enough to be thankful and take good care of them.

Mama also didn't tolerate any fussing or fighting among us. She wanted us all to get along, love each other, and be peaceful together.

Both of my grandmothers, in their own way and unique example, provided the light of God's instruction, which pointed us toward being connected with God on a sacrificial love and spiritually enlightened basis. Thereby we could be empowered to act and live "right."

And we could demonstrate the evidence of God's authenticity and righteousness on earth in our daily lives. We could then hopefully lead others to him in the expectation of the soon-coming kingdom of God through Christ Jesus.

But how could we accomplish this in our natural humanity or in connection with the world? We couldn't. We had to be directly connected and living by the indwelling Holy Spirit of God.

Only by this spiritual relationship with God—this method or vehicle provided by God—could we fully begin to understand and comprehend the mysteries of God's wisdom revealed in Jesus. We could subsequently look forward to the future revelation of all the eternal riches of God's kingdom through, of, and in Christ, glorified.

First Corinthians 2:9–14 (NKJV) affirms this clearly by teaching us,

> But as it is written: "Eye has not seen, nor ear heard, Nor have entered into the heart of man—The things which God has prepared for those who love Him." But God has revealed *them* to us through His Spirit. For the Spirit searches all things, yes, the deep things of God. For what man knows the things of a man except the spirit of the man which is in him? Even so, no one knows the things of God except the Spirit of God.
>
> Now we have received, not the spirit of the world, but the Spirit who is from God, that we might know the things that have been freely given to us by God. These things we also speak, not in words which man's wisdom teaches but which the [*Holy*] Spirit teaches, comparing spiritual things with spiritual. But the natural man does not receive the things of the Spirit of God, for they are foolishness to him; nor can he know *them,* because they are spiritually discerned.

God used both of my grandmothers from diverse perspectives to somehow communicate something far beyond the normality of our human experience and the incomprehension of our natural mind. They pointed us to the spiritual provisions and connectedness of God's Holy Spirit. Thereby, we could begin to live within the essence of God's wisdom—his true wisdom.

Both of my grandmothers transitioned into eternity by the time I was a young man. And I'm truly sad to say that not everyone in our family received and actuated what was being modeled, communicated, and offered through them by God—though several did.

But those who did, including me, have a spiritual connection with the love and wisdom of God. It equipped us to at least begin to embrace the infinite nature of God's mind, which inspires us to seek, perceive, and experience our lives and life everlasting through God's eyes.

CHAPTER NINE
PURSUING THE MIND OF GOD

THROUGHOUT ALL HUMAN HISTORY, THERE have been endless ventures by those striving to test the limits of human-centered ingenuity and grandeur. There have been countless endeavors to extend the boundaries of human strength and endurance—and expand the capacity of human domination and perception.

But in so doing, these undertakings have also acted to aggravate the scope of God's patience. These have included ancient examples recorded in the Bible, such as the Tower of Babel, (Genesis 11), Nebuchadnezzar and the three Hebrew boys (Daniel 3), the Egyptian dynasty (Isaiah 19 and Exodus 1–12), and others.

Modern-era examples include the many sponsored expeditions up the tallest mountains, voyages across and under the deepest seas and oceans, and treks across vast lands and wildernesses. This innate human drive has led to countless journeys to remote parts of the earth to witness and study wildlife, culture, and nature—hopefully to attain new scientific advances and historic discoveries.

In fact, scientists of all stripes have conducted exhaustive studies of the mysteries of the human body, the human mind, the environment, the atmosphere, and outer space with its countless galaxies, trying to unlock their many hidden secrets. But some of the most interesting and contentious pursuits have been among philosophers, archeologists, and other scientists who study a composite of information trying to define creation.

The typical scientific approach to almost everything is to immediately exclude the reality of God and rely solely upon the extent of human intellect to explain the existence of whatever they observe which actually subsists on a level far above their heads. This becomes a little strange after a while, since it's the creation trying to trade places with the creator, to then examine, understand, and explain what the creator did, without even acknowledging the actual existence of a creator. Now, try saying that at top speed five times in row…

Another analogy would be trying to understand a red Ferrari parked out in the middle of the desert and attempting to explain how it amazingly came to be, without acknowledging any help or design from human engineering to create and build it. But the good thing is that God already knows us and how we think—which is why he tries to save us some valuable time and serious frustration.

Philosophers, and particularly those who are atheists, are my favorites. I learned a lot about them when I studied philosophy in college. Many of them seem to go through the most excruciating exercises trying to explain away what they can't explain or understand.

However, I do believe the fictional detective Sherlock Holmes finally got it right way before several of them did. He concluded that "when you have eliminated the impossible, whatever remains, however improbable, must be the truth."

At the center of the human struggle to be relevant, both to one's self and others, they have neglected to see the simplicity of reality's truth. They have chosen to chart extravagant courses around it by setting out on adventurous quests and mighty challenges—even though the greatest adventure of all has been staring them right in the face from the very beginning.

So, why is it so difficult for us as human beings to accept our inability to accept our inabilities? Perhaps it's because we imagine ourselves as being destined for greatness, which we are. However, we can't relate to that involving our need for something or someone else greater that exists outside of ourselves.

This is quite interesting since that need for purpose and accomplishment is a distinctive quality and drive that God himself instilled within us. Perhaps initially it was for survival and procreation.

But then it was primarily to pursue our supreme development and maturity. And maybe the most difficult thing for people to understand and accept is that the ultimate completion of our maximum growth and maturity can only be reached, fulfilled, and solely appreciated in God.

There's nothing wrong with being ambitious or having big dreams. I know that I certainly have my share. But there's a problem when you can't objectively evaluate your situation, confess your human limitations, and then proceed to seek competent assistance existing outside of yourself. It's like you're pushing aside God (the creator of all things), and saying, "Hey, get out the way! You don't know what you're doing! I'll do it myself!"

But at the core of this problem is perhaps the introduction of the philosophical movement "Humanism" into our society. The *Oxford English Dictionary* describes Humanism as "an outlook or system of thought attaching prime importance to human rather than divine or supernatural matters."

"Humanist beliefs stress the potential value and goodness of human beings, emphasize common human needs, and seek solely rational ways of solving human problems." It exists as an antidivinity, antitheism, "nonreligious" movement.

Human-centered philosophy is nothing new. It has been around in one form or another since about 1500 BC. However, over the years it has developed into a formal movement, which has now grown and expanded into recognized religious establishments, associative organizations (nonprofit in some cases), and political groups that use their power to lobby the government in support of their views and goals.

Nevertheless, one solemn quote that has always stuck with me is "No man is an island." This quote originates from the English metaphysical poet John Donne (1572–1631). It suggests to me that we're all connected to that which is greater than ourselves.

And therefore, it's perfectly normal for people to require help that falls outside of their resources and power alone. David in Psalm 61:2 (NIV) cries out in distress, "From the ends of the earth I call to you, I call as my heart grows faint; lead me to the rock that is higher than I." It's time to look up to a higher source when we need help, or when we're trying to accomplish anything substantial—at least the really big things in life.

Well, the absolute biggest thing there is in life…is *life*! And upon examining some of the great philosophers and big thinkers of our age, I have found that some have wisely chosen to admit or at least provide an analysis for when they have arrived at the end of their human intellect and understanding—while still avowing their desire and search to learn and know more.

And the only way to know more about everything is by pursuing the mind of God, the source of all there is to know. And even from a humanistic perspective, seeking knowledge exclusive from God may be their solemn intention. But the only way to conduct that search is by surrendering to the God-given opportunity and the human faculties with which he has equipped them to do so.

Probably the most compelling argument for anyone to overcome when conceding or denying the existence and power of God's mind at work, is the undeniable evidence of "design" in creation. This is where both philosophers and atheists have trouble trying to sustain any reasoning they may have to the contrary. This also goes back to the example I gave earlier about the "red Ferrari parked out in the middle of the desert."

Another similar hurdle for those who may have resolved to prolong their denial of the existence of God, or his direct involvement with creation and humanity, is found in their writings or other historical accounts. These testimonials suggest an instinctive awareness or acknowledgment of God and his nature. They even seem to recognize God's "goodness" and ensuing influence demonstrated in examples of human virtue, truth, knowledge, and ethical behavior.

Romans 1:19–20 (NIV) speaks to both of these arguments very clearly: "Since what may be known about God is plain to them, because God has made it plain to them. For since the creation of the world God's invisible qualities—his eternal power and divine nature—have been clearly seen, being understood from what has been made, so that people are without excuse."

Therefore, it's not surprising there would be at least a few cases wherein philosophers may have initially held to the supremacy of human knowledge, and atheists may have refuted the existence of God, and then somehow experienced a change in revelation, understanding, or basic conception of God. Perhaps they discovered flaws in their own final analyses, based upon realities that they could not explain or could no longer ignore.

Among the list of philosophers that come to mind are some very well-known names, including Confucius (551–479 BC), a Chinese philosopher. Though he didn't believe in a being like the God of the Bible, according to the Classroom. Synonym.com article, "Who Is the God of Confucianism?," he did believe in "a force called the Tao, also known as the Great Ultimate. Confucius believed that the

Tao was the impetus for creation and that this force flows through all life, enabling change and betterment."

Socrates (470–399 BC), a Greek philosopher, was considered to be a "moral philosopher." The History.com article "Socrates" states, "Although he never outright rejected the standard Athenian view of religion [*of his day*], Socrates's beliefs were nonconformist. He often referred to God rather than the gods, and reported being guided by an inner divine voice."

Also, as stated in the Wikipedia article "Socrates," he asserted that "while so-called wise men thought themselves wise and yet were not, he himself knew he was not wise at all, which, paradoxically, made him the wiser one since he was the only person aware of his own ignorance." Socrates was executed by the Athenian government, being "found guilty of both corrupting the minds of the youth of Athens and of impiety," and also for "not believing in the gods of the state."

Plato (420s–340s), another Greek (Athenian) philosopher (and also a devoted follower of Socrates), as stated in the Wikipedia article "Plato," he has been credited as "one of the founders of Western religion and spirituality." Plato considered "The Good," which some claim was a direct reference to God, as the supreme Form, somehow existing even "beyond being."

Aristotle (384–322 BC), also a Greek philosopher, was a student of Plato. Beyond his many contributions to Western culture—philosophy, science, music, politics, economics, ethics and much more—Aristotle wrote significantly about what he observed and studied about nature (a level of understanding that Romans 1:20 supports). In his article, "Aristotle's Concept of God," Stanley Sfekas, Ph.D., says, "Aristotle conceived of God as outside of the world, as the final cause of all motion in Nature, as Prime Mover and Unmoved Mover of the universe."

Emanuel Kant (1724–1804) was a German philosopher. In his 1763 book (1799 edition), *The Only Possible Argument in Support of a Demonstration of the Existence of God*, Kant argues from the viewpoint of "design," and "the organizational structure of the universe," and the need for "an absolutely necessary being," and ultimately "the concept of God as a Supreme Being, which 'embraces within itself everything which can be thought by man.' 'God includes all that is possible or real.'"

Frederick Douglass (1817–1895), as an African American social reformer, abolitionist, orator, and writer, "Being exposed to many religious sermons as a child, he eventually converted to Christianity." "Early in his activism, he often included biblical allusions and religious metaphors in his speeches," as stated in the Wikipedia article, "Frederick Douglass."

"Although a believer, he strongly criticized religious hypocrisy and accused slaveholders of wickedness, lack of morality, and failure to follow the 'Golden Rule.' In this sense, Douglass distinguished between the 'Christianity of Christ' and the 'Christianity of America' and considered religious slaveholders and clergymen who defended slavery as the most brutal, sinful, and cynical of all who represented 'wolves in sheep's clothing.'"

Among the atheists who became Christians are such names as Francis Sellers Collins (born in 1950), an American physicist-geneticist who discovered genes associated with several diseases, including cystic fibrosis. According to the Wikipedia article, "Francis Collins," he considered himself to be an atheist until his eventual conversion to Christianity, which began with a process of conversations with other believers leading "him to question his lack of religious views."

Collins then began to study the "evidence for and against God in cosmology" and read the book *Mere Christianity* by British writer/lay theologian C. S. Lewis, also another former atheist. "After several years of deliberation, he finally converted to Christianity during a trip to the Cascade Mountains."

But one of my favorite examples is Lee Strobel (born in 1952), a lawyer, an American Christian author, and a former investigative journalist. Though an atheist, following his wife's conversion to Christianity, Strobel began to investigate biblical assertions using his investigative skills and expertise as a lawyer and journalist. Upon reviewing the compelling evidence, which he authenticated using standard legal "rules of evidence," he became convinced of the truth and became a Christian.

These examples demonstrate our human need to legitimately pursue true knowledge and our ability to eventually find it. God is both the source of and the object of what we're seeking, even if we don't know it. I'm sure that might seem like a paradox.

But God openly presents himself as the source based upon his own self-revelation—through nature, through creation, and by the many writings about him (including the Bible). Consequently, missing God in nature would literally be "missing the forest (or in this case, the 'forester') for the trees."

These writings have been inspired by God to be recorded by people who have personally encountered the knowledge and understanding of God on many levels. But the most significant of these levels is through Jesus Christ, the revealed Living Word of God.

Therefore, true enlightenment is only achieved by God's deliberate pursuit of humanity to know him directly, and for humanity to ultimately know the spiritually discerned mind of God. This is the greatest understanding of God and life itself—the personal connection of humanity to God's ageless presence and incalculable elements of wisdom.

Although God has gone through great lengths to achieve this connection, he must still distinguish the difference between humanity's sincere desire for true understanding in God, and the corrupt human covetousness to usurp God's power and authority and replace God's wisdom with their own. First Corinthians 1:25 (NIV) speaks to this by declaring, "For the foolishness of God is wiser than human wisdom, and the weakness of God is stronger than human strength."

This begins to explain the scope of God's mind, which exceeds our capacity as humans to comprehend. It also speaks to our lack of spiritual authority (outside of Christ) to sit in judgment over things, but especially the human impulse to sit in judgment of God.

First Corinthians 2:15–16 (NKJV) explains, "But he who is spiritual judges all things, yet he himself is *rightly* judged by no one. For 'who has known the mind of the Lord that he may instruct Him?' But we have the mind of Christ."

And, in Isaiah 55:8–9 (NKJV), God further explains, "'For My thoughts *are* not your thoughts, Nor *are* your ways My ways,' says the Lord. 'For *as* the heavens are higher than the earth, So are My ways higher than your ways, And My thoughts than your thoughts.'"

Therefore, the central theme from what we've seen is that in the pursuit of knowledge and understanding, there is a divine relational strategy at work. God has authenticated in his word that in similar fashion to Solomon (which I'll talk more about later, in chapter 12), he is pleased and willing for us to have access to his wisdom, just for the asking—as long as we respect and understand the spiritual nature and realm of God and his desire for us to trust him.

When we examine the historical writings and accounts of philosophers and others and compare them to the modernistic compulsion of the human need to learn, what's clearly at work here is an exchange or collaboration of incentive. In other words, from within the human spirit God has placed this innate desire to search nature, and the cosmos, and all creation for answers to satisfy our intense craving for knowledge and understanding.

While from God's perspective he has also placed himself and everything he has created in plain sight for those seeking knowledge and understanding to study and eventually find. It's all right there for anyone to see and to move toward to satisfy that need—that drive for obtaining wisdom.

Jeremiah 29:11–13 (NIV) puts it this way: "'For I know the plans I have for you,' declares the Lord, 'plans to prosper you and not to harm you, plans to give you hope and a future. Then you will call on me and come and pray to me, and I will listen to you. You will seek me and find me when you seek me with all your heart.'"

This intentional strategy designed by God brings mankind and God together to reach the same goal. That is the mutual connection between God himself and humanity within the realm of his divine purpose.

So, please understand that the goal of attaining enlightenment via God's spiritual wisdom is never to know everything there is to know just like God. We are never to aspire to be God. Well, there was that one guy, Lucifer, but you see how that worked out.

None of us could ever become omniscient like God, even if he literally tried to load everything he knows into our minds. Just like with a computer's limited capacity, we would always need to add more and more terabytes of memory. It would never be enough. It would never be possible.

We also wouldn't know what to do with all that knowledge even if we had it. I'm certain that God is the best at what he does as the creator. He's far more experienced and qualified than any of us could ever be.

But the real goal is to be a joint heir (Romans 8:14–17)—a spiritual beneficiary of all that God knows in the experience of his eternal glory and in the joy of his boundless nature and understanding.

This allows for the best of both worlds—having access to all knowledge and all wisdom in God, without having to be the vessel that contains it. Again, that's impossible for us even as the redeemed spiritual children of God. For he alone is infinite. We're not.

CHAPTER TEN

SHIFTING TO A CHILDLIKE WISDOM— A SUPERNATURAL POWER

Going back to my childhood, it's vital to remember that children have a special quality that unfortunately tends to diminish gradually as the years go by. They have an innocence that acts like a sponge and allows for the effective nurturing and teaching of crucial principles.

These principles include learning vast ideas in very productive yet simple and concise ways. Tragically, these same ideas elude many adults.

They have been bombarded with all kinds of masked social biases and intricate (and somewhat redundant) hoops to jump through in their thinking. Adults regularly underestimate the magnitude of what's critical while giving unwarranted devotion and overreaction to the insignificant.

So, let's look at another favorite subject of mine: dessert! Who among us does not love a big thick, moist slice of chocolate cake? Anyone?

I imagine there are a few lonely souls that have unfortunately become full-fledged, card-carrying members of that miserable fan club and motley crew that dislike chocolate. I can't imagine why. But it may give pause to reflect upon their level of wisdom in that important matter.

Nonetheless, for those who do love chocolate cake, most people who indulge in such decadent desserts do so for the sheer experience of enjoying the amazing taste and sensory satisfaction of just eating cake. You take in the aroma, which then triggers your immediate salivation and cravings, which then completely take over.

Even just hearing the words "chocolate cake" sparks an instantaneous reaction of exciting expectations. But beyond that, once you begin to eat the cake, every bite, every morsel passionately arrests your taste buds, which leads the way to a pure sensory overload of happiness and delight! Okay, I hope I at least grabbed your attention just a little bit by now.

So, maybe for you it's some other exciting delicacy…I don't know—maybe ice cream or pie or tiramisu or something…Anyway, just go along with me here with the cake theme.

Now try to imagine enjoying that big piece of chocolate cake along with someone who upon tasting the cake, fixes his or her attention completely on trying to figure out each and every ingredient and every single step in the preparation and baking process. Would that make any sense to you? Would that be normal? Of course not!

Our human focus is normally on living the complete experience in the moment, rather than lending ourselves to the tedious exploration of all the minute details. But we actually learn so much more about what's important and valuable to us by simply experiencing something or enjoying someone's presence, rather than trying to dissect them.

Another couple of examples also come to mind. It wasn't until after my parents passed away that I really got to know some of the more private details about them—things revealed in file cabinets, in folders, on paperwork, in desk drawers, etc. For instance, my parents never really liked talking about their age. Their age? Their business!

So, when the subject ever came up when they were living, they would discreetly deflect from the subject probe. This was when other people tried to inquire. My brother and I may have been curious at times, but honestly my mom's and dad's ages weren't a dealbreaker for either of us. Whatever it was, it just was. Cool!

Even as a child growing up, the only real major thing for me was my parent's presence in my life and their relationship with me. That was the level of data and grasp that I needed and expected from them. Anything else beyond that was basically trivia and had very little impact.

That's not to say that I wasn't interested in or involved with the unique details of my parents' lives. In fact, they were very interesting people! Things such as their likes and dislikes, their personalities, their interests, and their preferences were all great things to learn and talk about.

Also, the activities in which they participated; their jobs, faith, and church; their music; times when they were concerned or sad about something; and things that made them happy were all important. But those also were things we all learned about each other in the total experience of living together, and by just being a family in each other's presence.

And of course, as they got older, I had to eventually face the fact of their impending health issues. I had to then address other kinds of details that would ultimately impact me and the status of their daily presence in my life forever.

But otherwise, I had what I would consider a childlike faith and understanding of who my parents were. That was more than enough for me. I felt loved, provided for, safe, appreciated, important to them, valuable to them, and celebrated. And I felt like they really enjoyed my company and just having me around in their lives.

Now, this leads me to interject a slight pet peeve of mine, which may seem like I'm contradicting myself a bit. But I promise I'm not.

I've encountered a lot of ministers and pastors who emphasize and campaign for a virtual eleventh commandment—to memorize and consume a bunch of scripture, learn Christian faith apologetics, study all types of discipling techniques and strategies, attend Christian schools and seminary, learn the original Greek and Hebrew languages, and lots of other things.

And all of these things are very, very important—especially if you're addressing the need or preparation to witness to someone, lecture on the subject of theology, or become a Bible teacher. Or maybe you've been called to preach or evangelize for the purpose of winning souls and developing disciples for Christ. All of this is actually quite amazing. I get it!

I also really appreciate all the work and valuable information that Bible historians and scholars along with biblical apologists and research teams have done. They have excavated, examined, and dissected all of the details of ancient biblical artifacts, archeological findings, and foundational evidence to authenticate scripture and other important pillars that support the Christian faith and the reason for our beliefs.

In fact, these same people go on to develop and write biblical theses, books, concordances, Bible dictionaries, Bible translations, Bible commentaries, study guides, topical writings, and much more than I could ever absorb. And again, all of these are resources I have used on occasion that are essential, especially when preparing to do the work of building up the kingdom of God.

Nevertheless, I have to pause and offer a word of caution here from my own experience. Most people in this world are just "average Joes," and they themselves may never reach this level of biblical understanding and wisdom in one lifetime. I'm not saying they shouldn't try. But it's difficult as life happens to us.

And I'm sure that if someone did nothing else in his or her life (from birth to death) but read and study the Bible and all of the world's Christian resources and information it has to offer, he or she would still never learn everything there is to know about God. It's humanly impossible!

In fact, it's impossible to learn everything just about what Christ did when he walked the earth. In reference to the disciples writing down and recording all of the events and details of Jesus's life and deeds, John 21:25 (NIV) explains that "Jesus did many other things as well. If every one of them were written down, I suppose that even the whole world would not have room for the books that would be written."

So, what am I saying? I'm asking what is it that God cares about more than anything? How does God want us to spend much or most of our time? What does he desire of us? What is God's overriding emphasis, which is clearly reflected in the Word of God and in Jesus's coming? What is it that seems to matter to God above all else? And what does God's heart feel and reveal?

Well, there are some good clues and examples that point to what God is getting at. Scripture seems to focus mostly on four main dynamics:

1. Understanding the true meaning, purpose, and power of the Word of God versus just knowing all the words without understanding or embracing the meaning;

2. Knowing God by spending time in his presence versus spending time doing great tasks for God without knowing him;

3. God's love for children in their pure pursuit and acceptance of spiritual wisdom versus wholesale endorsement of human wisdom from an adult/self-centered perspective; and

4. The unyielding yet simple faith and trust in Jesus, God's son, the incarnate Word of God, Savior and Lord, even in the face of peril and death.

Let me expound further on each of these:

1. So, we know that Jesus rebuked church leaders of his day for being hypocritical, arrogant, and prideful about all the laws and holy scriptures they knew, without truly understanding their meaning, power, and significance in terms of obedience (Mathew 23). They even added new policy restrictions and rules that were unnecessary and superfluous to what was already stipulated in the law. Yet they failed to obey and even follow those requirements themselves, while hypocritically lording them over the people.

    But the biggest offense was that when Jesus was standing right there before them all, the incarnate Word of God, in their human wisdom, wickedness, and selfish pride they denied the very presence of God in the person of Jesus Christ. They denied who Jesus was and had him crucified, even though the scriptures of which they were supposed to be ordained authorities clearly foretold his coming in the manner that he came.

2. We can also get a picture and gain great insight from an account in scripture regarding Mary and Martha (Luke 10:38–42 [NIV]). Martha was busy preparing a meal for Jesus, who was visiting them. Martha got upset and angry with Mary, who was spending time with Jesus by sitting at his feet. She called out to Jesus to rebuke Mary.

    But Jesus lovingly admonished Martha instead, for her being so busy doing so many things while he was right there. Jesus commended Mary for choosing to experience the "good part" or "what is better, and it will not be taken away from her."

This was the more important thing, which was gained from spending time, fellowshipping, learning, and acquiring spiritual wisdom directly from the source, Jesus Christ, right there in his presence. In this example this rare opportunity came against the looming backdrop of his imminent crucifixion.

Isn't it interesting that God consistently demonstrates that he really wants to know us and for us to know him more by spending time in his presence? That intimate experience sitting at the feet of Jesus tells us more, and offers an opportunity to embrace spiritual wisdom in a way that could never be acquired by feverishly filling every waking moment with activities or work—even by memorizing every Bible verse, or jot and tittle of scripture. Prayer, meditation, praise, and worship are always great ways to approach God and spend quality time with him.

But also, sitting at God's feet involves watching God working in people's lives and in the force of nature. God gives us all a front-row seat to observe and learn how he thinks and moves and handles the countless situations in life and in the world, both good and bad.

Examples of his wisdom are truly endless and are like sweet fruit on the vines of untold orchards, reaching far beyond the horizon. And to taste and consume from this vast sea of fruit and nectar is not just for pleasure, but also for our continuous spiritual nourishment and development.

3. Now when it came to children, Jesus was adamant about their role and how they were at the heart of his focus and God's mission in the world. Mathew 21:14–16 (NLT) says, "The blind and the lame came to him in the Temple, and he healed them. The leading priests and the teachers of religious law saw these wonderful miracles and heard even the children in the Temple

shouting, 'Praise God for the Son of David.' But the leaders were indignant. They asked Jesus, 'Do you hear what these children are saying?' 'Yes,' Jesus replied. 'Haven't you ever read the Scriptures? For they say, "You have taught children and infants to give you praise."'"

Then, Psalm 8:1–2 (NLT) conveys what's central by declaring, "O Lord, our Lord, your majestic name fills the earth! Your glory is higher than the heavens. You have taught children and infants to tell of your strength [*Greek-to give you praise*], silencing your enemies and all who oppose you."

I believe this really speaks to the amazing power and wisdom of a child's untainted praise and connection to God through unadulterated faith and sincere understanding. As adults, we should all seek that level of wisdom with humility to honor God and defend his name.

I want to also point out one other key factor here, regarding conversion to a childlike perspective of spiritual wisdom. When children are born into the world, they concede to trust and depend totally upon their earthly human parents for everything they'll need to live and learn as human beings. Well, the same goes for when a person is born again as a new babe in Christ: they learn to trust and depend completely upon their heavenly spiritual parent, the Lord, for everything they'll need to live and learn about their new life in Jesus.

4. Finally, a person's life doesn't always allow for or need all the bells and whistles desired to exhibit a strong testimony of faith and wisdom. Our faith must be pure and simple, but also expedient—which is made possible due to a profound recognition and endorsement of who and what Jesus is as Savior, but also with the utmost trust and expectancy of his everlasting shelter and provisions as Lord.

This kind of faith is established only by a spiritual connection to God. The biblical account of the repentant thief on the cross displays this purity of faith and wisdom in action, even in his rebuke of the other thief.

Luke 23:39–40 (HCSB): "Then one of the criminals hanging there began to yell insults [*began to blaspheme*] at Him: 'Aren't You the Messiah? Save Yourself and us!' But the other answered, rebuking him: 'Don't you even fear God, since you are undergoing the same punishment?'"

I believe in verse 40, a case can be made for the word "fear" having a contextual double meaning or application—the thief being frightened or afraid of the impending death sentence, which the other thief is about to face for his deeds, just as he is. But it can also have the connotation of him not reverencing or respecting Jesus as God and Savior—who by the way is able to save him too, if he only believed.

In either case, with the thief insulting Jesus as he does, he's definitely missing the point and an opportunity of a lifetime, literally. But the repentant thief is both accepting the gift of salvation while bearing witness to the other one, who is spiritually blind. The repentant thief's wisdom is validated in his humble but powerful request to the Lord, for him to remember him, and in Jesus's promise of eternal life to him that very day.

Luke 23:41–43 (HCSB): "'We are punished justly, because we're getting back what we deserve for the things we did, but this man has done nothing wrong.' Then he said, 'Jesus, remember me [*Lord*] when You come into Your kingdom!' And He said to him, 'I assure you: Today you will be with Me in paradise.'"

CHAPTER ELEVEN

REEXAMINING THE RELATIONSHIP OF FEAR AND WISDOM

As I mentioned previously, Psalm 111:10 (NLT) clearly teaches us that "fear [or reverence] of the Lord is the foundation of true wisdom. All who obey his commandments will grow in wisdom. Praise him forever!"

Although there can be an innate transition from fear to wisdom, true wisdom requires discernment of how fear and spirituality interrelate. The experience of pain for the first time produces a negative dynamic and a tangible human response, which then causes fear (or us becoming frightened) to occur. Fear then produces a permanent understanding within our conscience that connects the action or source of the pain to the captivating feeling of fear.

That understanding yields a type of respect for, and the refraining from that source of pain, which initially created the feeling of fear in the first place. This negative fear cycle logically supports the human side of wisdom, but not the true wisdom cycle of God.

As human beings we tend to trust the wisdom we acquire from human experiences to navigate life without God's involvement or direction. Human wisdom can be helpful at times, but it can only take you so far.

On the other hand, when it comes to the wisdom of God, the fear cycle works somewhat in reverse. The fear of God is produced by his relationship with us in a positive empirical setting, as demonstrated by his perpetual love extended to us, his close fellowship with us, his faithful provisions for us, and his fulfilled promises in us.

Our parental relationships are a "type" or symbol—a mirror which reflects that "fear of God" model. So, just like we're not frightened of our parents in the surface sense of the word, we also don't fear God as being frightened of him, because we know him and he knows us.

Therefore, the progression would be more like, we fear or respect God because of who he is, and who he is to us. Based upon that relationship we seek to live by his spiritual wisdom (his word, his teachings, his warnings, and our understanding based upon our interactive experiences with him). We faithfully trust God and praise him accordingly. So, we refrain from whatever he has told us to avoid, and obey him by doing whatever he has told us to do.

But if we happen to disobey him, that would cause us to experience spiritual pain. And, depending upon what we've done or failed to do, it may also result in physical, tangible, emotional, or mental pain, as a consequence of our sin and corresponding behavior.

This would then lead us to become fearful or frightened. But remember that "God has not given us the spirit of fear," so this would go against our spiritual nature.

Therefore, as we become frightened, we become distant from God, which would motivate God like a good shepherd to lovingly seek us, forgive us, and then discipline us for the purpose of our redemptive restoration back to himself. But also, that disciplinary pain of God's own design would teach us as a practice to return to him, seek forgiveness, and refrain from further disobedience.

Then our spiritual response to God would be that of love, gratitude, joy, and praise. And the memory of this entire occurrence would be imprinted upon our spirit and conscience, as a permanent reminder of God's goodness, rather than that of any terror or pain.

Therefore, our desire would be to grow further in the spiritual wisdom of God, become more obedient, and seek to avoid similar incidences in the future, which would grieve God's heart and cause him to experience pain as well from our actions. (This is how I felt when I disobeyed and disappointed my parents—like I grieved their hearts and their goodness by not obeying them.)

So, the cycle of God's spiritual wisdom is now complete, at least in terms of our earthly existence. The fear or reverence of God is the foundation and catalyst toward obtaining and living in God's ageless spiritual wisdom, as well as knowing its treasures, which are immeasurable in life and in the richness of truth.

Ultimately, the spiritual essence of God's wisdom cycle culminates with his face-to-face meeting with us in perfect understanding and ceaseless expression of love, personally and eternally. First Corinthians 13:12 (NLT) tells us, "Now we see things imperfectly, like puzzling reflections in a mirror, but then we will see everything with perfect clarity (Greek, *see face to face*). All that I know now is partial and incomplete, but then I will know everything completely, just as God now knows me completely."

CHAPTER TWELVE

YOU HAVE NOT BECAUSE YOU ASK NOT—WHERE IS YOUR WISDOM?

So, how many of you remember growing up and asking for something that you really, really wanted—especially something good that only your parents could provide? And then you had the answer abruptly come back, "No!"

The "noes" of life begin very early. And in some ways they set us up for some major confusion when we get older.

But I must say in full disclosure the number of noes for me were far less than those for my older brother, Dehrric, at least at first. He kind of became my "no" lightning rod, so that I only had to watch the glaring sparks light up from what happened to him, and then learn my lessons vicariously and rather quickly.

The word no just doesn't sit well in our spirits when we hear it. That's mainly because when the no is delivered, it comes most of the time with a sharp attitude and a sourpuss expression on the messenger's face.

And in my experience, I don't remember getting many smiling or laughing noes—as though the no was really a good thing for me that I should be overjoyed about. Probably if I had, I would have assumed the person was relishing in my painful denial, in some sort of sick and sadistic kind of way.

But as you grow older, you learn to appreciate the blessing of no—as a means of protection from something not so good for you. And the longer you live, you realize that a strategically placed no could be a way to avert you from something that's not necessarily bad for you, but doesn't represent what's best for you, either—neither in the short term or for your long-term success.

So, the trick is planting some seeds to harvest what you think is in your best interest. It's sort of like that game kids play with their parents around Christmastime, or around their birthday, when they're trying to feel their parents out, to see what they may be willing to buy for them. Now, this is obviously for kids who don't believe in Santa Claus—at least, not anymore.

But they do things like make up cute songs about something they saw on TV that they want. Or they start repeating the name of a toy or a game or an electronic device over and over again—saying how much they'd really love to have it. Sometimes they even find clever ways to make whatever it is part of a typical family discussion.

Something like this: Mom says, "We really need to get out of here so we can get to church on time." Kid says, "You know, that new iPhone I saw that just came out last Friday has this really cool alarm on it. I know that would help me—I mean *us*—to wake up better." Or they just go old school and start pointing it out every time they go with you to the store.

But none of these tactics will work, because Mom and Dad already have in mind what they plan to get. Or they've already gotten what you wanted and are just letting you squirm a bit in childhood ignorance.

Regrettably, sometimes as adults we try to play those same childhood tricks and maneuvers on God when we want something from him. We drive by the car dealership and boldly point out that sports car on the lot that just happens to be in the color we really love, and say things like, "Wow! I know God is gonna get that one for me someday soon. Hallelujah! I have the faith! Yes, I do! Thank ya, Lord Jesus!"

And we do this hoping God will overhear us and maybe get it to us through our spouse or friend. Or perhaps he'll miraculously drop it down from heaven, right in front of our house one morning, already paid for with the keys in it, engine purring like a kitten. Well, if that's all you're looking for from God, he may just give you exactly what you want.

But if you're looking for something bigger, quicker and better that has a much greater chance of God giving it to you, try asking for some "wisdom." James 1:5

(NKJV) lets us know, "If any of you lacks wisdom, let him ask of God, who gives to all liberally and without reproach, and it will be given to him"

In fact, King Solomon in the Bible, who could have requested anything he wanted from God, asked him in 1 Kings 3:9 (NLT), "Give me an understanding heart so that I can govern your people well and know the difference between right and wrong. For who by himself is able to govern this great people of yours?"

Then God not only gave Solomon the wisdom he asked for, but he gave him something even more precious, his commendation for making the wisest decision he could have ever made—to request what was in his best interest, and moreover, in the best interest of God. Spiritual wisdom is what God wanted Solomon to have even before he asked.

First Kings 3:10–12 (NLT) confirms that, "The Lord was pleased that Solomon had asked for wisdom. So God replied, 'Because you have asked for wisdom in governing my people with justice and have not asked for a long life or wealth or the death of your enemies—I will give you what you asked for! I will give you a wise and understanding heart such as no one else has had or ever will have!'"

So again, where is your wisdom? Have you requested of God the most precious thing he could give you besides his love—that which provides treasure beyond your ability to fathom or receive? Do you have not because you have neglected to ask God for wisdom?

There are no "noes" to be expected or feared from this request. Just ask! Mathew 7:7–8 (KJV) affirms, "Ask, and it shall be given you; seek, and ye shall find; knock, and it shall be opened unto you: For every one that asketh receiveth; and he that seeketh findeth; and to him that knocketh it shall be opened." This is one request you don't ever have to worry about it being God's will for you to have. It is!

And wisdom is much too precious a gift to leave lying on the table of God's goodness. The key involves no tricks or pretense or beating around the bush. God already wants us to partake of his spiritual wisdom. He wants it to change our lives in ways we can't begin to imagine. So, just ask in sincerity, and he will grant you your request!

CHAPTER THIRTEEN
SURVEYING WISDOM'S GLORIOUS TREASURES

WISDOM IS LIKE A GLORIOUS ship that sails the seas of life.

It carries on board its endless treasures that enrich the heart and mind. And all who board her become a part of her endowment to spend and share. For wisdom's ship belongs to all who would ask if they'd only dare. She never sails to faraway places and exotic lands to dock. She never seeks remote shores to bury treasures beneath the rocks. No plans to hide for later claims and for others never to find. For wisdom's treasures remain on board for her passengers throughout all time. ~ *Poem by Terrence Richburg*

Proverbs 3:13–18 (NKJV) affirms, "Happy *is* the man *who* finds wisdom, And the man *who* gains understanding; For her proceeds *are* better than the profits of silver, And her gain than fine gold. She *is* more precious than rubies, And all the things you may desire cannot compare with her. Length of days *is* in her right hand, In her left hand riches and honor. Her ways *are* ways of pleasantness, And all her paths *are* peace. She *is* a tree of life to those who take hold of her, And happy *are all* who retain her [*hold her fast*]."

So, what abounding treasures do we see? What riches do you gain and experience from obtaining, storing, valuing, and dispensing God's ageless wisdom?

1. Contemporary Happiness

2. Enriched Understanding

3. Untold Success

4. Heavenly Resources

5. Spiritual Wealth

6. Fulfilled Opportunities

7. Extensive Lifespan

8. Eternal Riches and Honor

9. Gratifying Living

10. Peaceful Journeys

11. Infinite Sustenance

12. Everlasting Joy

Solomon also exemplifies in 1 Kings 3:12b–14 (NLT) the multifaceted benefits of seeking and obtaining wisdom treasures: "I will give you a wise and understanding heart such as no one else has had or ever will have! And I will also give you what you did not ask for—riches and fame! No other king in all the world will be compared to you for the rest of your life! And if you follow me and obey my decrees and my commands as your father, David, did, I will give you a long life."

But moreover, the most amazing depth of understanding, yet the crowning jewel of all wisdom, is the gift of Jesus Christ himself. First Corinthians 1:30 (NIV) confirms, "It is because of him [*God*] that you are in Christ Jesus, who has become for us wisdom from God—that is, our righteousness, holiness and redemption."

And Colossians 2:2–3 (NIV) affirms Jesus as the embodied treasure of God's wisdom: "My goal is that they may be encouraged in heart and united in love, so that they may have the full riches of complete understanding, in order that they may know the mystery of God, namely, Christ, in whom are hidden all the treasures of wisdom and knowledge."

The sad thing is that despite these remarkable treasures and promises to be received from the wisdom of God, people still choose to reject them and throw away the opportunity of a lifetime and far beyond. But if you are one who sees not only the opportunity for wisdom treasures, but also the infinite value of God's gift of himself to you, in Jesus Christ, then you, like me, will choose what's best—the "good part," "what is better, and it will not be taken away…"

This is not based on human intellect or strategy. It is based upon your response to the calling of God's spirit and his wisdom that resonates within your heart and soul.

So, let me break it down to a vernacular that hopefully everyone will understand by saying this: refusing what God is offering would be the most regrettable thing you'll ever do. But accepting God's gift of himself is the wisest decision you'll ever make!

CHAPTER FOURTEEN
PRACTICAL WISDOM FOR A MODERN SOCIETY

※

It's still quite surprising how things stay the same over the years. History repeats itself in such a way that fundamentally nothing really changes. Ecclesiastes 1:9 (NLV) says it best: "What has been is what will be. And what has been done is what will be done. So, there is nothing new under the sun."

One thing has been true from the very beginning. Human beings are bent upon doing things their own way, no matter what.

They have resisted guidance from those placed in authority over them or even have refused assistance from people who possess experience and knowledge to share—wisdom that if followed and utilized correctly would produce a far more favorable result. But many times, they have just ignorantly chased the random impulses and musings of their own thoughts.

Scripture teaches us that our natural way of thinking is not qualified to be trusted. In fact, Proverbs 14:12 (NKJV) says, "There is a way *that seems* right to a man, but its end *is* the way of death." So, God lovingly reaches out continuously to bring us to a level of understanding that will produce great outcomes for our lives, while we're living and ultimately after we die.

But in the constant clamor of our daily lives, many people just don't hear God's faithful attempts to reach us. He tries to steer us clear of dangerous intentions or uninformed decisions, barren of any measure of the kindest reasoned restraint. And of course, anything profoundly deeper than that is outright rejected, as being some sort of controlling political entity or spiritual anomaly that can't be trusted.

But Proverbs 1:20–23 (NLT) tells us, "Wisdom shouts in the streets. She cries out in the public square. She calls to the crowds along the main street, to those gathered in front of the city gate: 'How long, you simpletons, will you insist on being simpleminded? How long will you mockers relish your mocking? How long will you fools hate knowledge? Come and listen to my counsel. I'll share my heart with you and make you wise.'"

How prophetic is this, as we reflect upon the current times in which we live? It's simple. God is waiting and ready to clear out the cobwebs and replace them with the knowledge and power of his wisdom. Why do people resist or ignore the call of God?

We're facing daily episodes of pandemic outbreaks, job and business losses, and personal finance and health crises. We're encountering social unrest and injustice, racial violence, natural disasters, and municipal and law enforcement cruelty and backlashes.

There are widespread protests breaking out all over, concerning everything that's going on and everything that isn't. It looks very much like every dam is breaking, spilling the scorching waters of misery all over the murky streets and neighborhoods of humanity in the entire world.

How can we survive these desperate and chaotically painful times in which we now live? Well, as I mentioned earlier, it's not like this is anything new. "There is nothing new under the sun."

So, why is it that while God's wisdom is marching in the streets right there with us, we simply ignore it? Why do we turn from side to side attempting to make everything better under our own inadequate ideas and declining power?

Unfortunately, it's the same old story that has plagued the human race from the beginning. We're naturally selfish and prone to follow our own paths even if they lead to destruction. We take our eyes off the warning signs and choose to follow the faulty wisdom of this world.

Society has chosen to praise the ones who set their own rules and create a false sense of security and power, based on nothing but human ingenuity and pride. Even when failure occurs, somehow the human response is to follow the age-old definition of insanity: "Doing the same thing over and over again while expecting different results."

But I believe that in the book of James, God provides a stern rebuke to this way of thinking. And he offers a solution to address and defy the power of modern society's attempts to pull us away from his authentic wisdom.

God identifies the true character of spiritual perceptiveness in action, and then he assesses the ultimate failings of human wisdom by comparison.

James 3:13–18 (NIV) presents an inquiry and then responds to this question:

> Who is wise and understanding among you? Let them show it by their good life, by deeds done in the humility that comes from wisdom. But if you harbor bitter envy and selfish ambition in your hearts, do not boast about it or deny the truth.
>
> Such "wisdom" does not come down from heaven but is earthly, unspiritual, demonic. For where you have envy and selfish ambition, there you find disorder and every evil practice.
>
> But the wisdom that comes from heaven is first of all pure; then peace-loving, considerate, submissive, full of mercy and good fruit, impartial and sincere. Peacemakers who sow in peace reap a harvest of righteousness."

This rich passage of scripture pretty much says it all. But as with most people walking with the Lord, I have also gained some personal nuggets of insight and wisdom from God. Based on some of my treasured experiences with Him, and some notable observations of the human condition, I'd like to share some of those insights. I offered several in my previous book, *Soul of A Poet's Heart*, which I'll use as a stepping-off point to list some new ones.

My hope is that these kernels of wisdom prove to be helpful in prompting you to examine and appreciate the awesome gift of wisdom God offers to all who sincerely seek his counsel—this made possible by and within his greatest gift of Jesus Christ. I have included at least one wisdom nugget for each year of the average age required for full retirement.

So, hopefully over the years you'll have the time to meditate upon each of them as I will. I know before long your own personal list of wisdom quotes will begin to develop and steadily grow—as you spend time with God and just live your life with Jesus at the center of your journey, leading the way!

1. God loves you perfectly, and there's nothing more you can do to make him love you any more than he already does.

2. No matter how much you deny the existence of God, meeting God for the first time will erase all doubt.

3. Lies are not information; they're just lies.

4. The sum of all wisdom is God. The subtraction of God is the sum of all ignorance.

5. Never underestimate the power of the individual.

6. When one plays with fire, the fire always wins the game.

7. Empathy doesn't require that you've gone through the same thing that other people have. It only requires that you're willing to be there for them when they do.

8. Keeping your mind on Jesus leads to losing yourself in his love.

9. Keeping your mind on yourself leads to denying Jesus in your sin.

10. Worshipping at the feet of a liar is worse than despising the very existence of truth.

11. Wishing for the reality of a counterfeit is like wishing your hundred-dollar bill was a forgery.

12. Refusing a blessing from God is the same as rejecting the air you breathe.

13. Changing your mind to what's right when you're wrong is praiseworthy. Changing your mind to what's wrong when you're right is pathetic.

14. Ignorance might surely be bliss. But wisdom is absolute peace.

15. The economy of Satan is based on 100 percent debt and 0 percent return. The economy of Jesus is based on 100 percent gain and 0 percent loss.

16. Being a racist is like a blind man hating the colors of the rainbow even though he has never seen them.

17. Having a conscience can get you through the church doors, but repentance can get you through heaven's gates.

18. Hate brings death to the living. But love brings life to the dead.

19. Work to live life, rather than living life to work.

20. Don't ever get married seeking to become complete in someone, or to complete that someone in you. Marry someone when you're already complete in Jesus, who has called someone to you, for you to add Jesus in you to that someone.

21. It has been said, "A bird in hand is worth two in the bush." I say two birds in the tree above your car are worth much to many at the carwash.

22. Teaching a child information will show her what to think. But teaching a child wisdom will show her how to live.

23. The success of your plans for tomorrow will be only as good as the faith of your prayers today.

24. Keeping your word is much more impressive than the eloquence of your speech to explain your excuses.

25. A small word of wisdom offered to a wise man yields far greater profit than many years of study by a fool.

26. It's far better to admit when you don't remember something and then be right than to insist you're right about something and then refuse to admit when you're wrong.

27. Deciding to vote against something you believe in only for political gain is like driving your car on the wrong side of the road and then complaining about the oncoming traffic.

28. Living inside a bubble only works as long as you have air.

29. Showering words of gratitude and acclamation upon your spouse during times of comfort reaps many deeds of appreciation and support during times of distress.

30. Choose to love, especially when it's difficult, so that when it's easy it will be automatic.

31. Worrying takes many hours away from living while cutting many days off your life.

32. Worship is thanking God for all he is. Prayer is asking God to make you more like him.

33. Knowledge is only dangerous when you believe you know more than the teacher and try to teach more than you understand.

34. A calm spirit breathes wisdom into a problem, while hysteria breathes confusion into your spirit.

35. Hating is such a waste of effort, especially when you consider how easy it is just to do nothing and achieve the same result.

36. A gift purchased from the store offers something special that fades with time. But the gift of yourself offers something that's one of a kind which lasts forever.

37. A song well presented creates a special moment in time to be remembered by many, but a poor performance creates the need for time for many to ask God for forgiveness for lying about what they've heard.

38. The truth will set you free, if in fact you tell it.

39. As long as someone believes he can get away with everything, he won't turn to God for anything.

40. Being "young at heart" is to feel the joyful optimism of childhood. But being young in spirit is to know the joy of being born again, a child of God by the blood of Jesus.

41. It's always important to understand your human limitations within yourself, so that you can experience your spiritual liberty within God.

42. Positive thinking is a wonderful exercise leading to great achievements. Thinking outside the box is an amazing adventure imagining all of the achievable possibilities.

43. Giving up for the sole purpose of appeasing someone is not wise, but giving in for the greater purpose of blessing someone displays great wisdom.

44. Guiding a child to respect others is essential for nurturing character, while teaching a child to respect God is critical for enriching a lifetime.

45. I'm often astounded at the extent people will go to avoid letting others see just who they really are, especially when everyone already knows and is just too afraid or too kind to tell them.

46. I have recently noticed the massive attempts of some to remake God in their own image. The problem is that they themselves can't measure up to their own set of moral values.

47. People shouldn't mistake God's long suffering and compassion for a lack of interest or awareness. God sees all and knows all and can move or remove when you least expect it.

48. The wisdom of a child seeking God far exceeds the intellect of a scholar lauding his own accomplishments.

49. Frustration is just God's way of convincing us not to ignore him and to consider doing things his way.

50. Living in the valley teaches us the peace of God, while living on the mountaintop teaches us the power of God.

51. Selfishness lies in wait to break the heart of relationships, while forgiveness stands ready to restore the bond of all our hearts.

52. It's better to do something smaller really, really well and have it turn out to be much better than you could have ever imagined, than to do something really, really big and have it turn out to be much worse than it should have ever been.

53. There's nothing like a world pandemic to force everyone to be in one accord with God and seek his wisdom. But somehow human pride always gets in the way of what God is trying to do.

54. The presence of the Lord never leaves those who abide in his grace, and the grace of the Lord never fails those who abide in his presence.

55. Procrastination acts like refined fuel for the engine of chaos. But patiently waiting on God for His guidance fuels the confidence to move in divine understanding.

56. Life has this nagging way of catching up with us all, no matter who you are and no matter what you do. It is at that moment when you have to choose who and what you will be, not only for the rest of your life, but also at the beginning of eternity.

57. You're not qualified to handle the job of waking yourself up in the morning—that's God's job, so, be grateful he's never on vacation.

58. A word of warning to the racist. Hating another race is your rebuke of God for His image and likeness not being worthy of your own, as though you have the right to judge the worth of God's creation.

59. Keeping track of your lies once you begin telling them is like trying to juggle live grenades. No matter how talented you are at keeping them going around, eventually they will all blow up in your face.

60. Giving of yourself to others is the one investment you can make that pays the greatest dividends to you without you ever needing to make a single withdrawal.

61. Believing that you're a self-made man or woman is quite risky. Everything might work okay at first, but when something breaks, you'll need to go find spare parts for repairs.

62. As a tree bends to overcome the strong winds of a storm, compromise in the heat of an argument will preserve the integrity of your purpose.

63. Kindness fills the cup of restoration, while greed breaks the dam of contempt.

64. Never get too frustrated when you're trying to lose weight. There's always going to be more to you than meets the eye.

65. Planting a few seeds of appreciation will harvest a great storehouse of devotion.

66. Do any among us possess the expertise to critique God's masterpiece, painted upon the fragrant petals of heavenly arrayed fields in springtime, or to criticize the personality of his splendor singing through the tinted leaves of glory in autumn's breeze? How then can anyone endeavor to shackle the very spirit of God's expression through the mosaic hues and virtuosic songs of his most precious creation?

67. The blessings of God are too abundant to comprehend and far too many for time to number. Better to choose to live with God so that you can experience them all at once forever.

68. What wisdom is there in a short life resting upon the lap of luxury, wealth, and ease when afterward you'll spend eternity toiling in the bowels of ruin, want, and anguish?

69. May the perfection of God's love be the source of all your strength, and may the power of God's faithfulness be the inspiration of all your joy.

*SOME WISDOM-SHARING TIPS: This is for those who may be called upon to impart wisdom and godly counsel to others. I've learned through my own encounters that some people may come to you requesting advice. And once you share the advice with them, they simply go on and do what they had planned to do in the first place. It's kind of like when you offer the gift of Jesus Christ to unbelievers. Some will accept the gift of salvation, and others won't.

As painful as that might be, I've tried to learn not to get offended or take it personally. But once you have done your part, the rest is up to God. Sometimes it just takes time for it to work its way down into their conscience and spirit, so that God can use the seed of what you've planted in them to begin to grow and change their thoughts from within. This will bring a permanent change of heart and produce evidence of that change on the outside.

Then there are times when God has already shared his wisdom with someone, and she's simply looking for someone else to either talk her out of it or talk her into it with some kind of spiritual confirmation. But it's wise to try to discern what's going on with them and follow God's direction. Lead with the purpose of never becoming the source of their confusion.

You can always encourage them to pray for themselves about the situation or seek God's guidance in his Word. Or you can humbly invite them to pray with you—so as to seek God's wisdom directly on whatever the matter is, or at least seek it with you interdependently.

Just remember that God will always answer your prayers one way or another when you earnestly seek him. And your sincere requests for God's assistance and wisdom will be granted unto you, which he will use to govern your life!

CHAPTER FIFTEEN
THE ANTI-WISDOM WAR MOVEMENT

It's quite frustrating for me sometimes when I watch the news on TV and see the extreme levels of misinformation and idiocy not only supported but applauded in our society. At times it appears some people are trafficking in borderline self-induced insanity.

Now, I know that some may feel that's a rather harsh judgment to make. But I dread that it's actually borne out by the evidence and may even be worse than what I have described.

It seems some people have just decided that they don't want to know truth or make informed decisions. They apparently love living in a synthetic bubble of personal reality, as alluded to in chapter 14 and so eloquently described in the 1742 Thomas Gray classic poem quotation "ignorance is bliss."

Everyone knows that when we were children, if we had chosen to act the same way some adults behave now, by deliberately disregarding truth and perpetrating deception, we'd all be in so much trouble, not only with our parents, but also with all our family members. We would be grounded forever, or have our mouths washed out with soap.

Or maybe we would have grown old in the corner serving out an endless timeout period. And of course, we may have experienced the wrath of that notorious switch. Moreover, we know that if any of our children ever acted like that, they'd suffer the same consequences.

So, what's happening? What in the world is going on? Hmmm, "the world"! Therein lies the lie and the answer. The world is just going along doing like the world does, when it does, what it does.

In all my frustration I realize that God has already prepared us for what we're experiencing. It all lines up with what is to be expected as witnessed, predicted, and warned about in scripture.

Isaiah 5:20-21 (NKJV) says, "Woe to those who call evil good, and good evil; Who put darkness for light, and light for darkness; Who put bitter for sweet, and sweet for bitter! Woe to *those who are* wise in their own eyes, And prudent in their own sight!"

Now, doesn't that sound very familiar? Haven't you seen something on TV that looks and sounds exactly like what Isaiah is describing? Of course you have! We all have!

That's because we're currently in a war with what I like to call the "Anti-Wisdom War Movement." The AWWM is a relentless evil attack against God's authority and wisdom, that has been going on from the beginning of the world.

It's a spiritual attack by the enemy, Satan, upon knowledge and spiritual wisdom specifically—and against the truth and authority of God. The enemy has been waging this war for ages with a plan to fabricate and capitalize upon the spiritual blindness and illiteracy of truth that runs rampant among the people of today's society.

Now please understand that when I use the words truth and wisdom together, I'm not necessarily using them interchangeably. However, they do intersect and draw directly from each other when addressing the relationship between reality and knowledge, and also how they apply to grasping and experiencing life. You can see this clearly when comparing the formal definitions of the two words:

> Truth is "the body of real things, events, and facts" or "a transcendent fundamental or spiritual reality," whereas wisdom is defined as "the soundness of an action or decision with regard to the application of experience, knowledge, and good judgment."

Within the context of the dynamic relationship between truth and wisdom, spiritual blindness and deception are nothing new. There are so many biblical and historical references, including cases involving Adam and Eve and the serpent, Noah, Moses and Pharaoh, Joshua, Joseph, Jesus, the early church, slavery and racism, the holocaust, and so many more, too numerous to list here.

But just as it was back when Jesus physically came to earth and lived among us, one driving force and useful tool of Satan is the world's philosophical and political systems and institutions, and their subsequent evil ideologies. They generate a culmination of wisdom-less life that's ripe for disaster and destruction.

People are abdicating their moral and civic obligation to seek and revere truth and even to recognize the value of reason and civility. They've also become opponents of wisdom as a foundational mandate to address the universal needs of the individual and society as a whole.

So, what is the prognosis? We're living in a "postmodern" era (which I'll address later, more fully), wherein many people simply and deliberately choose to reject truth and wisdom. Some are electing to embrace what they know are lies and then bury their heads in the sand of contrived impotence.

We should be honoring and creating a legacy of integrity based on devotion to God's truth and understanding, as he has revealed it. But so many people have decided to worship at the feet of political ineptitude, philosophical absurdity, and religious heresy. They do this while militating against the eternal value of God's veracity and the infinite treasure of true wisdom's resolve.

So, explain why it is that when observing today's situation—the embracing of and genuflecting to the bold satanic attempts at mass deception and masked manipulation appears so obvious to some of us, while others jump headfirst (pun intended) into this sea of mindless fallacy?

Well, Ephesians 5:15–16 (NIV) says, "Be very careful, then, how you live—not as unwise but as wise, making the most of every opportunity, because the days are evil."

Evil is evil, but also very cunning. So, I bet you've heard the phrases "crazy like a fox" and "wise as a serpent?" These applicable phrases speak to the diametric battle for the survival of wisdom and truth in society, in which we are soldiers.

Although these phrases come from very dissimilar origins, they both refer to the strategy Satan uses to deceive people and also the mindset we as believers have to use as a tactic to overcome the plans and schemes of the evil one.

In addition, as believers in Christ we have something Satan doesn't. We have the power of God's protection and spiritual discernment. Our spiritual eyes are open to what is transpiring in the spiritual realm, which can't be discerned with mere human insight or understanding.

Ephesians 6:10–14 (NKJV) says,

> Finally, my brethren, be strong in the Lord and in the power of His might. Put on the whole armor of God, that you may be able to stand against the wiles (*schemes*) of the devil. For we do not wrestle against flesh and blood, but against principalities, against powers, against the rulers of the (*this*) darkness of this age, against spiritual *hosts* of wickedness in the heavenly *places*.
>
> Therefore take up the whole armor of God, that you may be able to withstand in the evil day, and having done all, to stand. Stand therefore, having girded your waist with truth, having put on the breastplate of righteousness.

So, how can we apprehend, then combat the AWWM? We must resist the urge to fight on human turf and terms. But rather, we must deploy both spiritual wisdom and spiritual discernment to protect ourselves and our children, and our families, and our society from any harm or evil indoctrination. We must also utilize the readily available protection God has provided.

There is also another important component to this movement and cultural war we must face. We live in a time when the power of communication has been expanded to proportions never seen before in history. It has been hijacked for the purpose of creating a "virtual" chasm to disrupt the natural flow of wisdom from one generation to the next.

There are some other important facets of wisdom that are defined as "the body of knowledge and principles that develops within a specified society or period" and "the teachings of the ancient wise men." Job 12:12–13 (NIV) teaches, "Is not wisdom found among the aged? Does not long-life bring understanding? To God belong wisdom and power; counsel and understanding are his."

The integrity and successful transmission of this important body of knowledge and historical teachings are in jeopardy. This is due in part to the massive cultural shifts we're experiencing regarding the lines and methods of communication.

In this twenty-first century, we're constantly encountering new terms, slang, symbols, icons, and phrases that are being introduced into society at such a high rate that even well-established dictionary systems are having a hard time keeping up. And to think I used to have trouble just keeping track of new acronyms and their overlapping meanings.

But with the rise and onslaught of social media and hip-hop culture, this new language of merged pictorial symbols and scripted messages like "memes," "emojis," "hashtags," "links," "avatars," "texts," "tweets," and more are in a constant state of proliferation and flux with no end or slowing down in sight. This has even created the need for urban and social media dictionaries and guides for public reference.

Contemporary language deviations and substitutions are so rampant that I've personally witnessed confusion among those in the culture who create and propagate them. They don't always know which new terms, words, and methods are current or retired.

They also may not be sure about what meanings and definitions are applicable or inaccurate. I have even seen the adoption of old slang from former generations being repackaged and reintroduced into society as fresh new ideas.

So, let me be clear. There exists both a strategic advantage and a looming danger from this vast explosion of social media, cultural slang, and various technology-based methods of communication.

(Note: As a parenthetical let me break here for just a second. I want to express my deep concern about something I believe to be very unwise. Are you okay with turning over functional control and universal Wi-Fi and Bluetooth connectivity of your phone, your personal data, your home, your security, your computer, your TVs, your shopping, your schedule, your banking, your car—your whatever—to third-party company providers, to disembodied virtual AI talking assistants, with all these cute names like Siri, or Alexa, or Bixby, or Cortana, to do almost everything for you?

Now it's me who has that "ARE YOU CRAZY?" look on my face, like my parents did with me back in chapter 2. Technology, guys! It can and does malfunction. It can and does break. And it can most assuredly be hacked! Please, use your heads!)

That being said, on one hand these technological advances have created an extraordinary opportunity for mass dissemination of information and ideas on a global scale. In seconds anyone can communicate pretty much whatever they want to, to millions of people.

So, on the positive side, these advances have been extremely important tools to reach out to people with valuable knowledge, including wisdom-based assistance, impactful guidance, helpful tips, and even faith-based messages. They have also opened up profound dialogues with people across international borders with diverse beliefs and across organizational boundaries, leading to important advancements and benevolent achievements.

In fact, slang can convey a huge volume of contextual information and cultural expression by using a single term or phrase that resonates with the hearts and experiences of those tuned into that particular network frequency. I get it!

But the downside is that the prevalent nature of slang has created a brand-new form of exclusive language or lingo, which sometimes makes it more difficult for older and modern generations to communicate and network effectively. If older people want to communicate with their younger counterparts (even their own children and those growing up in this new generation), they will have to be proactive and learn to embrace this new language to bridge the gap. But this isn't easy to do.

And sometimes members of the younger generation pridefully misuse their intricate language and symbols to alienate members of the older generations, labeling them as being "out of touch." They may even manipulate it to be a hindrance or hurdle to learning or accepting the ageless wisdom being passed down to them, which they might regard as being of little or no value.

So, just as it's necessary for an older generation to reach out to the young, the younger generation must also learn to embrace the tried-and-true wisdom of their parents and ancestors. This is a wisdom that benevolently lingers above them like a thick silver cloud sheltering them from the rays of harm externally and internally, perhaps without their knowledge.

But unfortunately, there are times when this younger cultural mindset can be very stubborn. It seats them in a posture of having to learn about truth and wisdom from scratch, on their very own—rather than being able to take advantage of what the previous generations have to share.

Some may even argue that learning from scratch or on their own is better. This may sound good on the surface. But God's plan has always involved the passing down of generational wisdom as a way to reach, educate, and redeem his children.

So, without the benefit of time-tested wisdom, young people may miss out on learning some wise proverbs and stories that could help shield them from making really bad decisions. These decisions may result in disastrous and destructive consequences. Satan takes advantage of this dynamic by making it easier to introduce confusing and deceptive ideas and practices into the normal generational flow of wisdom building and the exchange of truth and trust.

One situation we're living through is this peculiar era of newly coined or adapted terminology, such as "virtual," "new normal," "social distancing," and many others that have risen quickly to a high level of prominence. As massive pandemics and social tectonic swings have occurred recently, they have changed the face of society in historic proportions.

We're also seeing the perpetuation of the iconic "streetwise" or "street smarts" philosophy. This alludes to the innate or adopted ability and need to fit in with street and urban lifestyles to navigate subcultural constructs.

As a product of a similar type of neighborhood or background, one is able to identify, empathize, and speak the indigenous language based on personal exposure to parallel experiences. These demographics can lend themselves to opportunities for constructive interaction, while still creating major barriers to generational acceptance and the necessity for bridge-building communications.

But then, we have to be quick to recognize the pervasiveness of subculture messaging, which tends to communicate through coded language and encoded symbols. It influences the social and many times spiritual mindset and behavior of its current and recruited members.

As a result, subculture messaging can entice participation in dark underground lifestyles and activities. This is especially the case if the person is inclined and susceptible to the nature of the content to which they're exposed.

Another version of this type of messaging is described as "dog-whistle" coded language or terminology. Just like a dog's keen hearing allows them to perceive and respond to the high frequency of the dog whistle, which eludes the less acute hearing range of a human being, a dog-whistle message is an "expression or statement that has a secondary meaning intended to be understood only by a particular group of people."

These are often political in nature and are meant to communicate certain viewpoints accepted or espoused by a political party or underwritten by a specific political or social platform. Many dog-whistle expressions are not only political, but are also used to communicate cultural and societal biases and prejudices, including racism and sexism.

Also, don't forget about "subliminal messaging" or "subliminal stimuli," which is a form of subconscious communication, of which the public was just made aware several years ago. These types of messages work on the subconscious level of the human psyche. They use brief imperceptible messages, strategically placed within many forms of audio and visual media. This includes cinema, radio, TV, music, and more.

As with other forms of communication, subliminal messaging can be used for something good, like helping people to learn new languages, lose weight, or kick bad habits like smoking. Or it can be used for something bad or questionable, like trying to fundamentally change or control someone's sincere beliefs, or motivating dangerous and destructive antisocial ideology and behavior.

And then there is this resurgence of terms like "my truth" or "subjective truth." These expressions and concepts speak to what is known as nonnegotiable truth based on one's own finite experience. In other words, if something happened to me or I believe that something occurred, then I can testify or attest to it being factual or true. On its face this could seem somewhat innocuous.

However, in our postmodern society, these terms can take on a more disturbing connotation that can promote a philosophy of "my truth" versus "your truth." In other words, a person's subjective truth can encroach upon not only the validity of the truth or experiences of others, but also the truth of reality in society itself—both in terms of the physical world and in opposition to cultural boundaries, laws, and accepted values.

This can also become hazardous to one's self and others, if extended out to its inevitable conclusion. An example of this belief system might be "It's my truth that drunk driving is okay." Or "It's my truth that (*as a child*) I don't have to follow the rules of my parents, and I can hang out all night, if I want to." This elevates one's opinion to the level of undisputable reality or relative morals.

Another kind of personal truth philosophy adopted by some is the sanctioning of "feelings" or "my feelings" to be the same as reality. This particular belief raises the level of "feelings" or one's own feelings about something to be equal with truth, or being a personal truth worthy of acceptance by others as fact.

This is despite evidentiary substantiation for it not being real. This can also become risky because of possible infringement upon the reality of another person's life experiences or liberty.

In other words, it can create the opportunity for something like false civil or criminal accusations or defamation of another person's character. An example might be, "I feel that that Black man over there was about to hurt me by the way he looked at me when I walked by."

This is applying subjective and often prejudicial biases based on one's own feelings, with no facts or evidence to support their assumptions. Another contemporary example might be, "I don't feel like following that order! It's all a hoax! I feel like I can't catch the virus if I go out and just hang with my friends. Nothing will happen to me…"

So, you may be asking, "What is the bottom line to all of this?" and "What caused these strange cultural shifts and unusual phenomena to occur in our society?" Well, the answer to your questions lies in a term I alluded to earlier, which indeed bears further scrutiny: "postmodernism."

According to the *International Education Studies*, vol. 8, no. 9, published in 2015, "A Critical Examination of Postmodernism Based on Religious and Moral Values Education," "Postmodernism," (*a new movement of sort*)

> born under western secular conditions, has the following characteristics: it emphasizes pluralism (*"a condition or system in which two or more states, groups, principles, sources of authority, etc., coexist."*) and relativism (*"the doctrine that knowledge, truth, and morality exist in relation to culture, society, or historical context, and are not absolute."*) and rejects any certain belief and absolute value; it conflicts with essentialism (*"a belief that things have a set of characteristics which make them what they are."*), and considers human identity to be a social construct; it rejects the idea that values are

based on developmental realities and also rejects the essential influence of human actions on human destiny.

This study further clarifies that while modernism emphasizes realities and the discovery of realities, postmodernism emphasizes the instability of everything and the creation of realities. Modernism believes in certainty, necessity and meta-narrative *("an overarching account or interpretation of events and circumstances that provides a pattern or structure for people's beliefs and gives meaning to their experiences.")*, while, in the postmodernist view, under no circumstances should any mention of these categories be made.

Particularly in the area of values, moralities, politics, and education no mention should be made of universal and constant theoretical foundations. Values are relative things that differ from culture to culture. Therefore, the postmodernism movement is actually the era after modernism and a type of transition from it.

So, in the writing style of Shakespeare had he been alive today, now doth the alluring lights turn abruptly upon our wits, with obtuse illuminations in the middle of this dark night. Wake up everybody! Now can't you see why things have gone off the rails the way they have?

"Modernism," "modern history," the "modern period" or "the modern era," which is what most people like you and me are familiar with, spans from about the year 1500 to present day. But a natural overlap occurs with the introduction of the "postmodernism movement" or philosophy, which began roughly in the mid- to late twentieth century, around 1940—although the term "postmodern" showed up historically as early as 1870.

But the irony of postmodernism is that the nature of its own philosophy destroys the assertions of its prideful claims. In other words, if postmodernism argues against the existence of "absolutes" and "realities," then the certitude of its own reality is in jeopardy and can't be substantiated as a "real" thing, or something that anyone can or should legitimately support or believe.

Another irony is that in order to sustain the declarations of the postmodern mindset, advocates of the movement have to actually lie about the realities and absolutes that are obviously occurring with great manifestation all around them—as though the rest of us don't notice the truth—the eight-hundred-pound gorilla in the room, painfully struggling to break free from its obscured captivity within their ideas. And even more tragic than their dishonesty to others is their willful deception of themselves.

And for the final irony, for the sake of argument let's just say that everyone everywhere signed onto the postmodernist philosophy and wholeheartedly chose to live their lives accordingly. What would be the inevitable result? I think you know the answer. It would indeed be complete anarchy and chaos.

There would be no government, because everyone would individually govern themselves. There would be no laws because everyone would decide for themselves what's right and what's wrong, even as it relates to other people. And there would be no…Well, you can see where this is going. I think even postmodernists would ultimately agree, this would be an intolerably bad idea, and could never work.

But the fact is, postmodernism would never get to this point anyway, due to the remnant of God's righteous nature that's written upon the subconscious DNA of humanity—as having been created by God in his image, (Romans 1). In other words, someone would have the courage to stand up and yell, no!

Nevertheless, the postmodernist movement is real, and its exploitation of technology is its primary weapon of choice. It's very dangerous, and it seeks to question and erode everything pertaining to modern Western culture and societal beliefs and norms. This includes knowledge, truth, morality, values, wisdom, and most importantly, the very existence and nature of God.

The postmodernist philosophy is a tool that Satan has seized upon to confuse people and make them subscribe to beliefs that would surely cost them everything in life and drive them to an unfortunate end. And if you're paying close attention, you'll be able to recognize the signs of postmodernism gradually taking hold in our society, and slowly throughout the world.

On the same lines, there is one other "ism" that I need to tackle here—that being "racism." Although racism has been around for a very long time, I believe it to be especially prevalent in our current society. And, I also believe out of all the anti-wisdom movements, racism is perhaps the most divisive and by far the most perplexing and difficult to fathom.

I am truly at a loss for why any rational person in this day and age would still be an advocate for such an absurd ideology. How can anyone fail to recognize the presence of racism, or fight against it when they see and witness it occurring—either as a blatant act or systemically?

Sorry, but I can get a little fired up about this issue. During my lifetime I have personally been the victim of flagrant and systemic racism on several occasions. But without getting into what could easily consume the space of a separate chapter, or become another book entirely, let's just focus on the wisdom, or the lack there of, of racism. Here are just a few basic facts to ponder:

1. No one had or has anything to do with, or any choice in the matter of the race, color, or ethnicity of his or her birth;

2. No one has the ability to change his or her race, color, or ethnicity of his or her birth; and

3. No one has any control over his or her birth as to the socioeconomic conditions or place of origin regarding his or her birth.

The one who does have something, and in fact everything to do with these choices and circumstances, is God. Every soul/every person's spirit—that which makes every single individual uniquely who he or she is inside—is placed by God into his or her designated body, with whatever outward characteristics, and to whatever particular parents, and in whatever particular environmental, place of origin, and socioeconomic conditions that God chooses.

This means that every White person who is a White person from birth could have easily been born a Black person from birth, and vice versa. This also goes for any individual within any other ethnic or racial group.

These are divine choices and decisions far above any human desires, preferences, grievances, assumed level of authority, or presumed degree of entitlement. Only God in his sovereignty can make these determinations.

And God has made them all for everyone from the very beginning, when he created the world and human beings. Now, do you know of any case to the contrary? Do you think anyone was able to choose his parents and race beforehand?

Well, you might argue that people can do things like use artificial insemination, surrogate childbearing, or other techniques to achieve the conception and birth of a child. And you may even say that as humans we can certainly take a stab at controlling or manipulating some of the physical aspects and attributes of a child in advance of his or her birth.

But there is no one who can ever claim to have the power, access, or ability to place the soul and spirit of a child into any particular human body. Only God can do that.

So, just on the face of this debate, how can any individual belonging to a specific race, having nothing at all to do with what and who he or she was when he or she was born, proceed to judge, control, undermine, or overrule what any other person of another specific race is, or should be allowed to be or become?

What makes a person's ego or vanity rise to that level? What causes a person to believe they have the right or permission from God, the creator of all, to act in his stead and supersede his authority and his Word or will in any way?

I've often joked with my wife that if I were God, I would just randomly mix up everybody's race and economic status just for the fun of it—making all the Whites Black, and making all the Blacks White. I'd even make all the poor and middle-class people become rich, and make all the rich people become the poor and the middle class, and so on. I might even switch them up over and over again whenever the feeling hit me, just to prove the point.

But that's one of the reasons why I know I wouldn't make a very good God. I would be thinking solely in human terms without the full capacity or benefit of God's knowledge and wisdom. God's thoughts and ways are on a completely different plain than that of any human being, no matter how intelligent or judicious we become.

So, then the question is, how wise can racism possibly be, in any form? Well, in looking at it from God's point of view, he already addressed it broadly in numerous scriptures from various perspectives in his Word—all of which are not good news for those who practice racism. I'll highlight a few of them here:

In Acts 17: 26 (HCSB) as discussed earlier, scripture establishes the sovereignty of God and his authority to place people on the earth how and wherever he wishes, by affirming, "From one man (*one blood*) He has made every nationality to live over the whole earth and has determined their appointed times and the boundaries of where they live." This scripture also puts to bed the notion of multiple "races" as such, since we all come from the same seed or bloodline—that being the human race.

John 7:24 (HCSB) clearly forbids the practice of judging people according to how they appear outwardly, by commanding, "Stop judging according to outward appearances; rather judge according to righteous judgment." And of course, a righteous judgment can only be done according to God's Word, as specifically revealed in the person of Jesus Christ, and under the authority and power of the Holy Spirit.

Also, when God was considering his choice of David becoming king over Israel, 1 Samuel 16:6–7 (NLV) reveals the mind of God on this issue: "When they had come, Samuel looked at Eliab and thought, 'For sure he is the Lord's chosen one who is standing before Him.' But the Lord said to Samuel, 'Do not look at the way he looks on the outside or how tall he is, because I have not chosen him. For the Lord does not look at the things man looks at. A man looks at the outside of a person, but the Lord looks at the heart.'" Wouldn't it then be wise for people to be in agreement with what God thinks?

And James 2:1–4 (HCSB) provides a very specific case for not discriminating against anyone:

> My brothers, do not show favoritism as you hold on to the faith in our glorious Lord Jesus Christ. For example, a man comes into your meeting wearing a gold ring and dressed in fine clothes, and a poor man dressed in dirty clothes also comes in.
>
> If you look with favor on the man wearing the fine clothes and say, "Sit here in a good place," and yet you say to the poor man, "Stand over there," or, "Sit here on the floor by my footstool," haven't you discriminated among yourselves and become judges with evil thoughts?

Galatians 3:28 (TLB) proclaims that for those who are in Jesus, we're all on an equal foundation as fellow believers, no matter what race, what ethnic background, what economic status, or even if you're a man or a woman: "We are no longer Jews or Greeks or slaves or free men or even merely men or women, but we are all the same—we are Christians; we are one in Christ Jesus."

And finally, Revelations 7:9 (NKJV) provides a vision of how it will be when all manner of people saved by the blood of Jesus Christ during the "Great Tribulation" period will be among those entering into God's kingdom: "After these things I looked, and behold, a great multitude which no one could number, of all nations, tribes, peoples, and tongues, standing before the throne and before the Lamb, clothed with white robes, with palm branches in their hands."

So, it's just not rational or wise from any human stance, and certainly not from God's viewpoint, that racism be given any weight or merit or purpose at all in God's plan. However, racism does add another tool to Satan's toolbox to wage war against God and his people—and in defiance of God's wisdom, which he pours out generously to those open to him seeking his understanding.

In conclusion, the Anti-Wisdom War Movement is real, and it's raging right in front of us. All of the above examples I've shared provide solid evidence that a wisdom solely based on human understanding, subjective thinking, and faulty opinions is neither trustworthy nor sustainable.

We must therefore swallow our human pride, return as "the prodigal son" to remain with God, and seek the stability and reliability of God's spiritual wisdom, discernment, and ageless truth to ensure our enduring protection and success. We need to be united under God, indivisible, or at least be willing to stand alone as individuals with God.

We have to be prepared and vigilant to fight against these subtle, but morally and mortally dangerous, attacks. These strikes are launched appearing to be harmless rockets and alluring fireworks by the evil one, yet designed to deflect, confuse, deceive, and ultimately destroy us.

CHAPTER SIXTEEN

SO, WHERE DO WE GO FROM HERE?—THE TAKEAWAYS

In light of what we've seen and examined concerning wisdom, it would seem like everyone in attendance at this modest literary gathering would simply consider wherever they are now in life, and by unanimous consent decide to move toward what's better and to where things are so much sweeter—as compared to their possible condition, position, and situation, presently.

You know, it's like when you're crossing the street and you hear and see that oncoming speeding car. It doesn't take rocket science to persuade you to move from where you are to where things are so much better.

In fact, I believe that would be nice even from God's perspective. He may just say, let's lay out all the facts, tell them the truth, present the evidence, and list the benefits, which obviously outweigh any possible harms.

Then let's wait for all the hands in the room to immediately fly up! And all of those who raise their hands and have decided to sign up for the exciting offer receive a supercool prize! No disclaimers. No small print. Just a wonderful prize with no strings attached!

Well, it's not that simple. People need to be allowed to make their own decisions. God has given us free will to make choices—good ones and even bad ones. And there are consequences to our choices and actions, some good and some bad. But the goal is to hopefully win some people over to what would clearly be the good side.

So, let's review what we've learned about wisdom treasures. What are the takeaways?

Do you happen to remember this game called follow-the-leader? I'm pretty sure most people are at least vaguely familiar with the game. But just in case someone isn't, follow-the-leader is a simple children's game in which all the available kids line up behind the chosen leader, and they endeavor to follow them wherever they go, and duplicate whatever they do.

There's no sense of democracy for the followers in this game. The followers don't have any choices or rights in the matter. The leader simply chooses his or her own path and randomly acts out anything he or she wants to do, and all the followers are supposed to do it.

I didn't play this game a whole lot. But when I did, it was at my elementary school. And it was quite entertaining, especially because we played it outside on the playground. Leaders of the line usually attempted to make the tasks they were doing harder and harder for the followers.

The point was that eventually followers would grow weary or frustrated and would not want to follow anymore. Or they'd lose the game because they couldn't follow successfully.

Otherwise, after someone stumbled or fell or did something else disruptive, and following the laughter that eventually died down, the rules allowed for someone else to take over the leader's position. And inevitably the new leader during his or her turn tried to move much faster and do crazier things to make it more and more difficult for the followers.

This was especially intended as a response to what the previous leader did. And now that I recall the game, I remember how much fun it really was.

But as we consider the current state of our nation and our world, one thing we know is that life is not a game. Some people treat it as such, but it isn't.

And what we have been experiencing in life recently as human beings is a lack of leadership. We are faced with multiple problems and concerns that have caused many people to become fearful and to lose hope for their future.

Some have become disillusioned with who they are. They wonder what, if anything, can change the direction of their impending pain and possible destruction.

But the main reason for this phenomenon is that many people have lost their way, or they have been negligent in their search to find it.

WISDOM TREASURES

Many have chosen to play the game of follow-the-leader in their own lives. And it seems that whichever way their leader goes, they follow.

They go right along without considering why they are following their leader and where they are going. And along the way they find themselves being forced or allowed to stumble, or to fall, or something else disruptive, that would cause a disaster to occur along their path.

Life is just too important to place it in the hands of someone or something that doesn't know anything about where it's going, or how to get you to where you need to be safely. So, let's consider another option.

What about choosing to follow the guidance of someone who knows everything about you, everything about the path, everything about the best destination, everything about how to get you there, and everything about everything else? Wouldn't that be a "wise" decision to make?

Wait! It gets better! Suppose this someone who knows everything is willing to teach you what he knows. Then, not only will you be wise to follow him, but he will show you how to be wise like him. Now, the choices and decisions you make will be good ones, because you're learning through your new experiences how to be wise.

Wait! It gets even better! Suppose that while you're learning how to be wise, and how to make good decisions, you're able to then teach your children, and pass on what you've learned.

So, now they can be wise, and they too will make better decisions like you've learned to do. And those decisions will be like the decisions you're now making, which are based on the knowledge and wisdom of the original someone that taught you.

I know that was quite a maze of twists and turns to get here. But getting to this result is the point and is possible for anyone. But it first depends on what or whom you choose to follow and to what or to whom you listen. Consider some of these takeaways:

1. The fear or respect of God is the foundation of all true wisdom.

2. God seeks the humble dependence and untainted trusting nature of a child's heart to reveal himself and successfully use the power of his timeless wisdom within the lives of his people.

3. Learning to respect and obey God involves experiencing pain, so as to confirm reality and avoid the consequences of bad choices.

4. Developing a yearning for true wisdom involves a process that combines personal experience with the applied guidance of parental instruction and the application of God's Word.

5. There are several types of fear, but being frightened is not of God and it serves no viable purpose when completing the mission and exercising the power of God's love and wisdom.

6. God's truth and wisdom are ageless and everlasting, and the treasures of wisdom are immeasurable.

7. The highest level and greatest treasure of wisdom is spiritual wisdom, which is obtained by the acceptance of the Living Word of God, which is Jesus Christ.

8. Human wisdom is limited and fails, but God's wisdom is true, powerful, infinite, and eternal.

9. The enemy or evil one, Satan, uses all kinds of strategies to undermine and attack the wisdom of God with human fear, confusion, and pride. But overcoming the attacks of Satan is accomplished through God's discernment and by the protection of God's spiritual armor.

10. Earthly human aspirations, political agendas, and communication barriers may be used to prevent or undercut the natural transfer and continuation of generational wisdom. But proactive engagement by older and modern generations alike provides remedial support for the inclusive communication of true wisdom and spiritually sound ideas.

11. God offers his spiritual wisdom freely to anyone sincerely seeking it.

12. The fulfillment of God's truth and wisdom is completed by the salvific plan for human life through Jesus Christ, and the final spiritual consummation of his eternal relationship with believers.

One other very important takeaway is trying to really wrap your head around who and what we're dealing with when we think of God—and the level of wisdom with which he's working. I believe one other reason why God's love for children is so strong and profound is that from their perspective, the world is way, way too big for them to understand on their own.

Adults even seem to be like "Marvel"-sized giants to children. And they're not on TV, but in real life. Regular objects and structures appear very intimidating as kids begin to compare their own size to what they see. It's all just too large to handle or comprehend.

Every small feat they achieve or every tiny new piece of knowledge or understanding they gain to them is what it feels like to celebrate graduating from college. This is because for them, it *is* just like graduating from college. To small kids, it all looks and feels like that big of a deal.

So, what do kids do? They cling to the things that make the world seem less ominous, which brings it way down to a place they can handle. Then they feel loved and connected and able to start to explore this brand-new world for themselves.

The warm arms of their parents and the peaceful room in their home is where it all begins to unfold. And it provides a wonderful launching point for their new adventure to commence.

Then as children grow and begin to take it all in—their environment, what they experience through their senses and innate perceptions—they become more responsive to the stimuli and information crossing the entranceway of their minds and spirit. They now become open to new perceptions and ideas.

Children are able to assimilate the newfound knowledge made available to them. And this opening of their minds in turn generates an open-mindedness. They can then receive and distinguish concepts and principles, some of which are rather complex.

Their minds and hearts are eager to learn more but also to participate in and understand what they've learned. Children are now capable of expressing their own beliefs and choices. They also have the ability to intelligently and intentionally respond naturally to the objects of their devotion and affection.

This is why the children recorded in Mathew 21:15–16 were able to act quickly and instinctively upon their understanding of who Jesus was. They offered their sincere praise and worship to him, while the adults were dumbfounded as to what was going on. The children's minds and hearts were in one accord with their understanding of God and the meaning of his presence.

But when it comes to adults, once we've grown up, we tend to be cavalier about things in our own attitudes, like "Been there, done that." We begin to lose that fresh innate excitement about every new discovery or precious bit of knowledge as it becomes real to us for the very first time. Nevertheless, when it comes to the universe and God, we are all still very much like that small child in the arms of our mom and dad, when we were first born.

Well, God is the only one that can credibly say, "Been there, done that." And it would be completely true! He is the one that has known the end from the beginning.

God is the one that is the essence of wisdom, having always existed from eternity past. Now, how can any of us begin to compete with that?

God stands ready upon the shores of perpetuity, beckoning to us to come hang out with him at his place, and in his world. In fact, God in the biblical appeals of "Wisdom" in Proverbs 8, and from Jesus in John 17 provides a comprehensive narrative and picture of his eternal plan and perspective for us, even way before any of us were born.

And then finally Ephesians 1:3–8 (NLV) clarifies beyond any reasonable doubt:

> Let us honor and thank the God and Father of our Lord Jesus Christ. He has already given us a taste of what heaven is like. Even before the world was made, God chose us for Himself because of His love. He planned that we should be holy and without blame as He sees us. God already planned to have us as His own children. This was done by Jesus Christ. In His plan God wanted this done.
>
> We thank God for His loving-favor to us. He gave this loving-favor to us through His much-loved Son. Because of the blood of Christ,

we are bought and made free from the punishment of sin. And because of His blood, our sins are forgiven. His loving-favor to us is so rich. He was so willing to give all of this to us. He did this with wisdom and understanding.

So, now how much wisdom do we need? Can we even begin to fully comprehend? Not really…Therefore, as for me, I just innately and simply respond by saying, "Praise God!" and recommend that we all "trust in him"!

CHAPTER SEVENTEEN
CHALLENGING QUESTIONS FOR CHALLENGING TIMES

1. What does the word "wisdom" mean to you?

2. What does the word "truth" mean to you?

3. What images and feelings does the word "fear" evoke in you?

4. Do you fear or respect God, and if so, how is that manifested in your life?

5. What is or was your relationship with your parents in regard to the level of respect you have or had for them?

6. In what way does wisdom play a role in your daily life activities and goals?

7. What individuals, past or present, have personally impacted your life with wise counsel or as a living example of wisdom?

8. If you have children, do they respect you, and if so, how is their respect demonstrated in your daily interactions with them?

9. What strategies do you use to engage your children in the building up of wisdom in and for their lifestyle experiences and plans?

10. What is the wisest decision you have ever made, and what did you learn from it?

11. What is the most unwise decision you have ever made, and what did you learn from it?

12. What practical steps can you take to improve the level of wisdom's positive impact in and on your life?

13. What role does God's wisdom play in your leadership style for your family or in other positions of authority or influence—e.g., work, business, church, etc.?

14. On a scale of one to ten, with ten being the best, how wise do you believe you are and why?

15. What recent experiences have you had that have taught you about the power of wisdom?

16. Drawing from the list I provided in chapter 13, what treasures of wisdom do you personally experience on a daily basis, and how?

17. What biblical personalities and their teachings and/or experiences have you learned from, relied upon, and modeled in your quest for spiritual wisdom?

18. What is your opinion about the value attributed to the concept and reality of truth and spiritual wisdom in today's society, as you see it?

19. What things would you change in the culture as a champion for elevating the knowledge and reliance of society's leadership upon God's wisdom and guidance?

20. What legacy do you want to bequeath to your family and others that would reflect the importance you've placed upon wisdom while you were living?

CHAPTER EIGHTEEN
JUST FOR FUN...

OKAY...ANYONE WHO KNOWS ME IS already aware—and maybe others upon reading this book will see—that along with the serious side of things, I love to mix in some jazz of the not so serious—some humor, which is a huge part of my personality. I constantly joke with my wife and my friends and family all the time, because life is already so serious and short lived.

I don't want to take myself too seriously, either. So, I want to bring a little levity to addressing the big picture. We have to lighten up sometimes just to keep from crying. But we also need to have fun, so that life won't feel overwhelmingly complex and severe.

We know that with everything that's going on these days, we really have to remain in constant prayer to make it through. But we also need to enjoy the gift of living within the abundant life God has already granted to us through Jesus Christ!

In fact, the spiritual wisdom of God affords us the assurance of his eternal peace, to freely experience the perpetual joy of the Lord, daily. And yes, we also have the gifts of our smiles and laughter with which to express the celebration of all God's blessings upon us!

So, this chapter of the book is entitled, "Just for Fun," and dedicated to just having a little fun while rejoicing in some scenarios I want you to try along with me. Nothing difficult; no pressure—just fun!

1. Singer-Songwriter—As I am a musician, singer, and songwriter, this idea comes straight from the heart: (a.) As a family or a couple, try writing a song about wisdom on the spot without using the word wisdom in the lyrics.

You can even use a familiar tune you know. Just change the lyrics to sing about wisdom—nothing "deep," just fun. Then share it with each other in a live performance. (b.) If you have children, try doing this as a rap or spoken word song. (Note: Feel free to use any instruments you may have lying around, even if you don't know how to play them. Or you can try using random objects in the room to improvise your musical accompaniment. (c.) And finally, consider recording a video of your performances on your phone for posterity's sake, or to share with loved ones, friends, or others on social media.)

2. <u>Speed Date</u>—For two or more people/group: Set up a game wherein you have thirty seconds to tell your spouse, friend, or your child everything you can about yourself. Then that person has thirty seconds to either repeat everything back to you perfectly, or to tell it to the next person in line accurately. With three or more people, the last person in the line has to tell the original person everything that was told to her perfectly. If she gets anything wrong, she's out of the game and loses. Then the next round starts with the next person in line. (Note: At the end of the game, feel free to correct any facts that were misstated or omitted—this is done in love, mind you. But also use this opportunity to talk more and get to know each other better.)

3. <u>Wise Guy/Not-So-Wise Guy</u>—For a couple or a group, each person has to share an experience wherein he would describe himself as acting wisely, along with what benefit resulted. Then he would share an experience wherein he behaved unwisely, along with what consequence occurred and what he learned...nothing really too personal or revealing about anyone. (Note: Most childhood stories are probably safe. Also, feel free to open up further discussion regarding each experience and how each person may have handled things differently, or even similarly.)

4. <u>Smart Chairs</u>—Play a game of musical chairs, and when the music stops, the person that gets blocked from sitting down has to spell and define a word from a prepared list of college-level words. If she doesn't know the real

spelling or definition, she will need to be as creative as possible and make up a spelling and a definition that sounds like something the word could actually mean. The group leader or participants can vote based on the player's accuracy or level of creativity to determine if she should be allowed to stay in the game.

5. <u>Wisdom Art</u>—Anybody like to draw or paint? Try creating an abstract picture or painting of what "wisdom" looks like to you. Try not to incorporate the literal word or its letters into your new masterpiece. Just use the imaginative impressions within your mind, based upon what we've examined and discussed in *Wisdom Treasures*.

6. <u>Comfort Texting</u>—Another thing I love to do is send out single or group texts to family, friends, and fellow parishioners that contain a favorite scripture of mine, or one that I believe will encourage those who may be going through a tough time—which right now seems to be all of us. You can do this too, but try using a scripture that shares something about the wisdom of God, which will hopefully bring comfort and peace to those that receive it.

7. <u>Wisdom Fishing</u>—Do an internet search of the Bible for any scriptures containing the word "wisdom." And then pick one or two from the list per day or per week (or whatever timeframe you choose) to meditate on and pray about. Then share your experience with your spouse, family, or friends, including what God has revealed to you from his Word. (Note: Feel free to include any of the scriptures used in *Wisdom Treasures*.)

8. <u>Wise Counsel</u>—Have a discussion with your spouse, a friend, or another family member about a fictitious problem or issue that could crop up in anyone's life—nothing major or particularly serious; e.g., maybe something like a bad grade on a school homework assignment or exercise, a stopped-up drain, a problem sleeping, a problem with boredom, an overbooked schedule, a traffic stop by a policeman, how to prepare a specific dish or meal, TV

programing/watching, etc. Pick and define the problem and then discuss ways to apply a wise approach to handling it. If you're comfortable using a real-life issue, that's fine. Just be careful when selecting your topic, so as not to touch a nerve. Remember this is for fun!

9. <u>Postmodern Scrabble</u>—Setup a game of Scrabble. But instead of playing using the strict rules of a normal game, setup your own crazy rules—e.g., a team against another team, accept words that aren't real words, have one player use one set of rules (maybe the correct rules), and the other player use his or her own set of rules, change the rules in the middle of the game, etc. You can also use this same approach to play Postmodern Checkers, Chess, or even card games. It should be quite hilarious! (Note: This should also work great to drive home the dynamics of how a postmodernist society would function, or not. Enjoy!)

10. <u>Live Emoji</u>—Have at least two people sit across from each other. Each person takes turns making facial expressions and/or exhibiting some type of body language. Use a pad and pen to write down what you believe or discern that particular expression or action means. Or you can simply have people yell it out. The person making the face or doing the action has to confirm whether or not the opposite player has gotten the answer right. You can also use props as available to display or augment your expression or action.

11. <u>Wis-Triv</u>—Try hosting a virtual Bible study in which participants discuss and study the wisdom of God in more detail. And then follow it up with a trivia game of related questions and fast facts to keep people engaged while still fellowshipping and studying.

12. <u>Student Aid</u>—Consider establishing a church- or community-sponsored scholarship to assist young students with their tuition or other expenses needed to attend college. One possible application or qualification prerequisite could be their submission of an essay (or an essay competition) that

addresses their personal views about wisdom, and its level of importance when approaching life and pursuing future success. (Note: You can also add a public element to the competition by having finalists read their essays to a selected panel or a public group for judging and voting. This could be either in a live or virtual setting.)

Now, I'm sure there are many other fun games or clever exercises and ideas you can come up with on your own. These provided here are only meant to help you and your family and others get started applying valuable lessons about God's wisdom to real-life experiences, while still having fun doing it.

Please have at it! I certainly don't have all the answers. But it's an honor and my joy to share what God has and continues to share with me, from his heart to mine, and from my heart to yours! Again, HAVE FUN! BLESSINGS!

CHAPTER NINETEEN
CLOSING THOUGHTS AND HOPES

My motivation for writing *Wisdom Treasures: Ageless Riches for A Modern Society* was simply to share some thoughts from my own experiences, as well as my personal excitement regarding God's spiritual wisdom. My life has been one of many ups and downs wherein God has shown himself to be a very real and present help in all times of trouble, and sometimes despair.

But over the years I found myself in situations wherein I was asked to share my advice and counsel, mainly in the area of my other love, music and the music business. It may have started off that way because people knew of my expertise and knowledge primarily in that area.

But I've also had a lot of other job experiences in which I was called upon to be in leadership, management, supervision, technical expertise, safety and security, strategic planning, equal opportunity and civil rights, and also the area of my spiritual giftedness, administration. And of course, relationships, family, and ministry always take you through some rather character-stretching exercises, both good and bad.

These diverse areas of my experience exposed me to a wide range of situational dynamics, which sharpened my aptitude for on-the-job self-development and total reliance upon God's leadership in my life—to both survive and excel. All glory be to God!

But along the way I found that friends, coworkers, family, associates, and recommended parties began regularly reaching out to me for guidance on some pretty serious life-navigating issues and personal problematic circumstances. And when those times came, I realized that I wasn't at a loss for words, and God revealed to me what to share.

I figured it was God just being God in that moment. And that was true. But I also realized that much of what I had to share came from the knowledge and understanding I had gained throughout my life. This process began from when I was just a child. It was amazing, humbling, and a little breathtaking to see God sowing wisdom in my life even from a very young age.

So, in my last book, *Soul of A Poet's Heart*, I was inspired to share an entire poetic chapter, "Culture of Wisdom," listing many of the profound insights of wisdom God had poured into me for much of my life. And then my close friend and encourager, Dr. Jerry West, upon reading that book and also another one I had written, expressed to me how it was such a blessing to him and his wife, as they both were going through so many extremely difficult health challenges together.

When Dr. West shared this with me, all I could do was humbly celebrate and praise God for using me and my books in this way. I was thankful that God had inspired me to bless someone, "literally" (pun intended), especially such a close friend.

But then even more recently, another dear pastor friend of mine, Bishop Al Way of Faith Assembly of Christ Church in Washington, DC, shared with me some thoughts he had regarding God's calling on my life that focused specifically on the subject of wisdom.

In fact, he mentioned from his interactions with me that he saw in me and my life a special calling and ability when it came to wisdom. Well, I was somewhat shocked. And honestly, I listened with a fairly skeptical ear and kind of tucked it away for later.

This wasn't because I didn't believe or respect what Bishop Al was sharing with me in terms of what he saw. But it was more like, Why would God use me in such a way, when there are so many wiser people than me in this world and in ministry that he could use, including Bishop Al himself!

But somehow it just kept gnawing at me and showing up again and again in my thoughts, and in my dreams. And God continued to pour into me words of wisdom, as I reflected upon all my past experiences, and especially as I prayed and constantly asked him for wisdom, as according to scripture. Well, it got to be so much that God finally inspired me to write this book, *Wisdom Treasures: Ageless Riches for A Modern Society*.

My hope is that someone, and preferably more than just "a" someone, will have fun reading *Wisdom Treasures* and be inspired to seek and possess the true wisdom of God, just as I have been. Believe me, there is no downside! God's faithfulness and his promises have all been amazing in my own life, but also in the ability with which God has blessed me to experience and share his spiritual wisdom with others.

There is no greater satisfaction than to be used by God for His purpose, especially when it's based upon his direct calling. So, I am forever humbled and blessed by what the Lord, Jesus Christ, has done and is doing in my life. All glory and honor be to God!

My other hope is that you and others will be able to experience that same joy of being used by the Lord, and that it will be at an even greater level than it has been for me, for the cause of Christ!

Blessings, always…
~Terrence

REFERENCES (ONLINE)

TheBibleGateway.com

    The New International Version (NIV) Bible

    The New Living Translation (NLT) Bible

    The New King James Version (NKJV) Bible

    The English Standard Version (ESV) Bible

    The Holman Christian Standard Bible (HCSB)

    The King James Version (KJV) Bible

    The New Life Version (NLV) Bible

    The Living Bible (TLB)

    TheNIVBible.com

BibleStudyTools.com

OpenBible.info

Biblehub.com

Wikipedia.org

Meriam-Webster.com

Oxford English Dictionary: oed.com

Phrases.org

Classroom.Synonym.com

History.com

Heptapolis.com: "Aristotle's Concept of God" by Stanley Sfekas, Ph.D.

The Only Possible Argument in Support of a Demonstration of the Existence of God by Immanuel Kant, 1963/1799 edition

"A Critical Examination of Postmodernism Based on Religious and Moral Values Education," *International Education Studies*, vol. 8, no. 9, 2015, ISSN 1913-9020, E-ISSN 1913-9039, published by Canadian Center of Science and Education, August 26, 2015

Bible.Knowing-Jesus.com

TERRENCE AND KATHY RICHBURG

Thank you, Kathy!

For your amazing love, patience, and devotion!

⌘

To my beautiful wife and angel here on Earth...

All my love,
Terrence

ABOUT *SOUL OF A POET'S HEART,*
AN ADDITIONAL LITERARY WORK BY
TERRENCE D. RICHBURG

SOUL OF A POET'S HEART
GALLERY OF POETRY, PROSE & SONGS

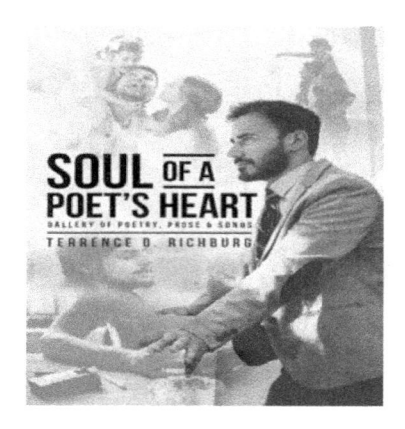

http://www.christianfaithpublishing.com/ books/?book=soul-of-a-poets-heart

https://www.youtube.com/watch?v=4MtVcImzpkk

Copyright © 2018 by Terrence D. Richburg.
ISBN: Paper Back 978-1-64191-345-4
Digital: 978-1-64191-346-1

Publication date: 08/13/2018
To order copies of this book, contact:
Christian Faith Publishing, Inc.
1-800-955-3794
832 Park Avenue
Meadville, PA 16335
www.christianfaithpublishing.com

ABOUT *INTIMACY,*
AN ADDITIONAL LITERARY WORK BY

TERRENCE D. RICHBURG

INTIMACY
MISSING "PEACE" IN THE PUZZLE OF
TRUE LOVE & CLOSE RELATIONSHIPS

http://www.intimacyrich.com/

Copyright © 2013 by Terrence Richburg.
Library of Congress Control Number: 2013909082
ISBN: Hardcover 978-1-4568-1382-6
Softcover 978-1-4568-1381-9
eBook 978-1-4568-1383-3

Rev. date: 06/13/2013
To order copies of this book, contact:
Xlibris Corporation
1-888-795-4274
www.Xlibris.com
Orders@Xlibris.com
83711

Terrence D. Richburg

ABOUT THE AUTHOR

Terrence Duane Richburg, Sr., is a contemporary Christian writer and author, and an award-nominated national gospel-jazz recording artist appearing on over 35 albums. He is an accomplished producer, arranger, composer, multi-instrumentalist, musician, prolific songwriter, lyricist, vocalist, orchestrator, engineer, musical director, and is sought after as an industry authority and resource for all things gospel-jazz. Terrence's musical roots stem from being the son of former Atlantic recording artists The Richburg Singers, and the nephew of the late jazz vocal legend Ronnie Wells.

Terrence Richburg is founder and CEO of RichEscape Music, LLC, a Stellar Award-nominated independent record label, production, and publishing company, which highlights his own unique style of music as well as other newly emerging talent, primarily in the gospel, gospel-jazz, inspirational, and praise and worship genres.

He has served in church leadership and ministry for over 30 years, up to and including mega-church level for all ages. He has ministered and served in church and music ministry and training at over 30 churches in the Washington, DC Area.

In the world of literature, Richburg is a gifted poet and freelance writer, drawing inspiration from God, who continues to pour Himself into Terrence as he walks with Him. Terrence is the author of the popular E-zine, JazzGospelCentral.com. His first book, Intimacy: Missing "Peace" in the Puzzle of True Love & Close Relationships was published in 2013 to wide acclaim, and was featured in the 2013 Frankfurt, Germany, and Guadalajara, Mexico, International Book Fairs, as well as the 2014 Book Expo America in New York. He published his second book, Soul of a Poet's Heart: Gallery of Poetry, Prose, & Songs, in 2018.

Wisdom Treasures—Ageless Riches for A Modern Society is Terrence's newest book. He has found that the more he writes and longer he lives, the more his experiences lead him to want to continue writing, and to try to help people with valuable lessons he has learned along the way. He hopes his writings leave a legacy that will live on to benefit others practically and spiritually, and perhaps to inspire others to become authors, too.

CPSIA information can be obtained
at www.ICGtesting.com
Printed in the USA
BVHW072304020921
615904BV00015B/2004